Femininities, Masculinities, Sexualities

The Blazer Lectures for 1990

FEMININITIES, MASCULINITIES, SEXUALITIES

FREUD AND BEYOND

Nancy J. Chodorow

THE UNIVERSITY PRESS OF KENTUCKY

Chapter 1 appeared in an earlier form in Jerome Neu, ed.,
The Cambridge Companion to Freud (Cambridge and New York:
Cambridge University Press, 1991), copyright © 1991 by
Nancy J. Chodorow. Chapter 2 appeared in earlier form in
Psychoanalysis and Contemporary Thought 15 (1992),
copyright © 1992 by Nancy J. Chodorow.

Library of Congress Cataloging-in-Publication Data

Chodorow, Nancy.
  Femininities, masculinities, sexualities: Freud and beyond /
Nancy J. Chodorow.
    p. cm.—(The Blazer lectures ; 1990)
  Includes bibliographical references and index.
  ISBN 0-8131-1872-7 (alk. paper)
  1. Sex (Psychology) 2. Freud, Sigmund, 1856-1939.
  3. Psychoanalysis. I. Title. II. Series.
BF175.5.S48C47 1994
155.3'33—dc20   93-39481

Contents

Foreword

Sigmund Freud continues to fascinate, irritate, and stimulate social thinkers a century after he initiated his psychoanalytic studies. Some credit him with having revealed to us the previously hidden dynamics of the unconscious, and they see his monumental discoveries as no less significant than those his contemporaries were making about the structure of the atom or relativity. Others—and this strain has been evident in some recent scholarship—blame him for opportunist, even craven, theorizing and sloppy, perhaps unscrupulous clinical technique. Freud's cultural and especially his gender biases have long been lamented. Critics of psychoanalysis argue that its propositions remain without significant experimental or epidemiological support.

Why, then, do Freud and psychoanalysis continue to draw so much attention? Nancy Chodorow's writings, including this provocative volume, begin to explain this interest. Chodorow, perhaps the preeminent theorist in psychoanalytic feminism, burst upon the world's intellectual salons a decade and a half ago with her pathbreaking *The Reproduction of Mothering*. In the years since, she has developed with increasing power her views on the intersections of gender, sexuality, and psychoanalysis.

In this volume, Chodorow examines two related questions: First, what role does or should difference or variation between individuals play in our understanding of psychoanalytic theory as related to sexuality—a typically (for Chodorow) bold question, since psychoanalysis has been handed down to us with what she rightly describes as "seemingly universalizing gender theories." Second, how should we understand the supposedly normative status of heterosexuality? Her answers to these questions are, again typically, surprising, controversial, and provocative.

Femininities, Masculinities, Sexualities grows out of Professor Chodorow's 1990 Blazer Lectures at the University of Kentucky. The Blazer Series, made possible by generous grants from the Paul G. and Georgia M. Blazer Fund and the Blazer family, have long enriched campus life, and we are grateful for their support.

Richard Edwards
Dean of Arts and Sciences
The University of Kentucky

Preface

In April 1990 I was privileged to present the Blazer Lectures at the University of Kentucky. As seems to be enduringly the case in my work, I reflected upon sex, gender, and psychoanalysis. This volume ties together some of those reflections. In particular, I address two empirical, ideological, and political issues that have concerned psychoanalytic feminists and feminist psychoanalysts in recent years. The first of these issues pertains to the question of difference and variation, against the seemingly universalizing gender theories of psychoanalysis. The second involves the normative status of heterosexuality in psychoanalysis and the historical uses of psychoanalysis in clinical, political, cultural, and ideological differentiating, excluding, and pathologizing alternative sexualities.

To address these questions, I investigate psychoanalytic constructions of femininities, masculinities, and sexualities. I read psychoanalytic texts through the lens of clinical experience to see whether these texts and this experience can yield insight into diversity and individuality which bypasses normative or universalizing conceptions. Through these investigations I hope to open up new spaces for addressing feminist concerns. My conclusions in the first two chapters rely mainly upon readings of specific psychoanalytic texts, but my increasing certainty about the importance of context, specificity, and personal individuality grows principally not from these texts but from my clinical observation of the extraordinary uniqueness, complexity, and particularity of any individual psyche. The third chapter draws indirectly upon this clinical experience, as well as upon readings that directly address cultural and psychological variation.

My approach begins with Freud. Chapter 1, "Rethinking Freud on Women," elicits from Freud's writings an alternative reading on the question of difference and variation. I suggest that Freud's writings on femininity in fact invoke and document clinical and social-historical diversity and specificity, and that Freud provided clinical documentation of variety and specificity in male reactions to women as well. Chapter 2 turns to the question of sexuality. An examination of theoretical and clinical psychoanalytic accounts of sexual orientation suggests that psychoanalysis does not provide grounds for pathologizing homosexuality except by tying heterosexuality to a culturally normative, male-dominant gender differentiation. Much as my 1978 book, *The Reproduction of Mothering*, questioned the cultural and social taken-for-grantedness of women's mothering, "Heterosexuality as a Compromise Formation" queries the psychoanalytic taken-for-grantedness—based on cultural and social normativity—of heterosexuality. Chapter 3, "Individuality and Difference in How Women and Men Love" brings together questions of gender and questions of sexuality as it addresses cultural and individual variation and specificity in women's and men's modes of sexual love.

I am grateful to Susan Contratto and Sherry Ortner, who read and commented valuably upon all these chapters. Elizabeth Abel and Joseph Lifschutz provided helpful suggestions about Chapter 1. The remarkable insight and sophistication of work on sexuality and sexual diversity by my students—Steven Epstein, Karin Martin, and Arlene Stein—made me self-conscious about my not having written directly on sexuality and inspired me to see what, in the context of their insight and sophistication, a rethinking of psychoanalytic approaches to heterosexuality could contribute. I formulated the argument of Chapter 2 in long discussions with Janet Adelman and Arlie Hochschild; I also thank Adrienne Applegarth, Steven Epstein and Ethel Person for comments, and Karin Martin for valuable research assistance, on that chapter. I owe a debt in Chapter 3 to the challenges of reconciling racial-ethnic, cultural, and sexual diversity with psychoanalysis in my teaching and, again, to my students who write and teach so well on these issues.

1   Rethinking Freud on Women

Psychoanalysis continues to vex and intrigue much of our thinking about gender and sexuality. In recent years, vexation has emerged from many sources. Feminist and gay and lesbian writers have challenged the normative masculinity, masculine bias, devaluation of women, homophobia, and heterosexism found in much psychoanalytic writing, as well as psychoanalytic clinical practice and politics in these arenas. They have also focused on putative essentialism and universalism in psychoanalytic theories, criticizing essentialism in the psychoanalytic assumption of two normative models of development— that of the girl and that of the boy—and in its pervasive and often unacknowledged biological determinism, and criticizing universalism in psychoanalytic tendencies to generalize about human, sexed, or gendered universals and to ignore or occlude cultural, racial, ethnic, class, and historical variation.

At the same time, most of these critics remain intrigued by psychoanalysis. No other major theory evinces such continual fascination with and attention to gender and sexuality and such a continual sense of how problematic, contradictory, overpowering, and complex these are—as experiences, as identities, as cultural constructions, as personal enactments. In reflecting on these vexations and this intrigue in this book, I consider how we might respond to, evaluate, and reconsider them. I begin with Sigmund Freud. Another look at Freud may reveal nothing new, but it may help us put our knowledge and observations together in ways new enough to let us acquire more complex psychoanalytic understandings of sex and gender and begin to reconsider the ideological and cultural underpinnings of these understandings.

Historically, psychoanalytic writing and everyday language have referred to "woman" as a unitary entity. Psychoanalysis has compared "the man" to "the woman," "the boy" to "the girl." Even discussions about "women" seem, in psychoanalytic writings as elsewhere, to refer to a single kind of woman. Recent feminist and poststructuralist writings have taught us to be wary of such singular referents and of theories that employ them. In particular, these writings criticize psychoanalysis for the limited class and cultural location of its clinical sample: that is, of the empirical "women" upon which psychoanalysis has developed its purportedly universal theory of femininity.

Such a reading comes, I believe, from a view that limits Freud's writings to his major statements on female sexuality, sometimes along with (deserved) criticism of the Dora case. When we interrogate Freud's writings, however, we find that his and others' psychoanalytic references to "woman"—the conventional account of female sexual development—are in dialogue with an emphatically plural account of a multitude of "women." Freud's descriptions of women and of his interactions with them involve a large cast of characters, a pantheon of greater and lesser ideal-typical goddesses and mortals to complement and accompany Oedipus, Narcissus, Moses, and others into psychological glory or ignominy. We also find actual, historically specific, late nineteenth- and early twentieth-century named and nameless women in clinical cases and vignettes. We come away from this wider reading with a more contextualized, situated, variable basis on which to construct psychologies of women, men, and sexuality. We also begin to unpack the context and situation in which Freud did his clinical work, and we thereby remind ourselves of the historical and psychological perspective and the pretheoretical assumptions from which Freud constructed his accounts. We do not make the universalizing, dehistoricizing mistake—reading psychoanalysis as if it has no personal, historical, or clinical specificity—of which we accuse Freud.

In enumerating the women that Freud discusses, I describe a number of implicit axes that differentiate them. As the conventional accounts and critiques affirm, in his "psychology of femininity" Freud describes woman—his patients, and the generalized developing girls, who are living experiencers of self and of conscious and unconscious mental processes—clinically and theoretically as psychological subject. I do not here mean to get into complex theoretical issues about the nature of subjectivity and its alienations and fragmentations; I mean, simply, what I believe we who are women ordinarily mean when we experience ourselves as "an I, who is female." Freud recognizes women as subjects in several different ways. Woman as subject expands into woman as subject-object: she becomes object to her own subjectivity as she internally relates to and identifies with or against another internally experienced woman.

Woman as subject or as subject-object contrasts with woman as object in the masculine psyche. Freud depicts for us clinically and theoretically how men experience women, and by examining his writings we ourselves can also find clues as to how men characterize women or imagine women to be. Freud also expands his investigation of woman as psychological subject or as object by considering woman's location in social-historical time and woman as object of cultural attribution or categorization.

Finally, Freud demonstrates for us a range of possible locations within the psychology and social organization of gender and sexuality. In his writings on sexuality and development, his cases, and his social theories, women

are young girls, mothers of daughters and mothers of
sons, daughters of mothers and daughters of fathers; they
are heterosexual, lesbian, sexually inhibited or frigid altogether; they are substitute mothers as nursemaids, ser-
vants, or governesses; they are wives, mother-symbols, or
whore-like sexual objects of desirous or fearful men.

This diversity stands as some response to the critique
of singularity. It suggests that although claims about
the limited class and cultural basis of Freud's patient
population may be largely accurate, we miss, by looking
only to cultural and social axes of differentiation that
inflect or intersect with the relations of gender, the very
great complexity and multiplicity of identities and social locations found within gender relations. Freud's
work on women is a good place to begin to delineate this
complexity and multiplicity.

Freud's writings on women have been contested from
the beginning. Both inside and outside the field of psychoanalysis there has been much revision, reformulation, challenge, and change, even though many psychoanalysts would still accept many parts or the whole of
Freud's writings on the subject. These new formulations
are beyond the scope of my concerns here.[1]

Nor will I repeat at length what I and others have
said elsewhere about Freud's limitations. I simply recall
briefly two glaring limitations—to use his own word,
scotomas—in Freud's account. First, the maternal—as
a strong, intense feeling, preoccupation, and identity in
women as subjects—is almost entirely absent, along
with adequate recognition or treatment of infantile attachment to the mother (my own earlier writings pay
attention to maternal identities and desires). Second,
hegemonic within his portrayed diversity is an account
of mature female desire and heterosexuality that ren-
ders them as inhibited at best; at worst, female desire
and sexuality are seen entirely through male eyes (chapters 2 and 3 address this latter scotoma).

Here I begin with woman as subject, a term by which I refer to what we normally mean by a self, actor, agent, experiencer. I am not concerned with contemporary accounts that problematize such a self or agent but simply wish to distinguish *in a general way* this psychological, social or cultural *subject* from an *object* seen or experienced by someone who is himself or herself the experiencing knower in an investigation or account. I distinguish five approaches to women as subjects in Freud's writings: first, theoretical woman in the developmental theory; second, clinical woman; third, woman as subject-object—theoretical and clinical woman as she herself internally represents and experiences woman as object; fourth, women as they are socially and historically located; and fifth, women as creators of psychoanalytic technique and understanding.

Conventionally, when we investigate Freud's writings on women, we are most concerned with the first approach, his developmental account of woman and femininity, of female psychology or sexuality. Reconstructing woman's development from adult clinical cases, Freud observes and interprets her subjectivity as a generic femininity. His account, then, along with most early psychoanalytic accounts, is about "clinical" girl and woman as Freud reconstructs her development from a life narrative constructed through transference and interpretations. It is not an account of "observed" girl, observed from infancy by analysts or developmental psychologists. As Daniel Stern points out, psychoanalytic theorizing that begins from clinical reconstruction tends to be "pathomorphic and retrospective."[2] That is, it retrospectively singles out conflictual adult clinical issues as overall definers of normative childhood phases and stages of development, as well as of central personality and identity issues throughout the life span. This girl or woman whose development Freud retrospectively describes is not empirically clinical; she is not an actual patient or patients. Rather, she is

Freud's theoretical feminine subject, or theoretical subject of theoretical femininity.

As is well known, Freud describes his theory of woman's development, or the development of femininity, in a series of articles written and published during an approximate ten-year span from the early 1920s to the early 1930s: "The Dissolution of the Oedipus Complex," "Some Psychical Consequences of the Anatomical Distinction between the Sexes," "Female Sexuality," and "Femininity."[3] In addition, Ruth Mack Brunswick claims that her account of the "preoedipal phase" is based on typed notes taken after discussions with Freud in the early 1930s.[4]

In these writings Freud subsumes what we now call gender, or gender identity, under sexuality, or sexual identity. "Femininity" and "female sexuality" are thus equivalent and what psychoanalysis can presumably concern itself with. As Freud puts it: "I have only been describing women in so far as their nature is determined by their sexual function. It is true that that influence extends very far; but we do not overlook the fact that an individual woman may be a human being in other respects as well."[5] The "normal femininity"[6] that is the preferred outcome of female sexual development is a heterosexuality entailing passivity and centering on the vagina as organ of sexual response and excitement. To achieve this normal femininity a girl makes three shifts in her development: from active to passive mode, from "phallic" (or clitoral) to vaginal aim, and from mother (lesbian/homosexual choice) to father (heterosexual choice) as object.

Freud developed his theory of femininity in two stages. In "The Dissolution of the Oedipus Complex" and "Some Psychical Consequences of the Anatomical Distinction between the Sexes," he begins quite explicitly from a male norm and compares female development to it. His discussions of female sexuality focus on the girl's originary phallic sexuality, her castration complex, and the

simplicity of her oedipal configuration: "The girl's Oedipus complex is much simpler than that of the small
bearer of the penis; in my experience, it seldom goes beyond the taking of her mother's place and adopting of a
feminine attitude towards her father."[7] Her castration
complex—envy for the penis—leads up to her Oedipus
complex; the Oedipus complex is never given up in as
absolute a way as is the boy's, because she has no castration to fear. Upbringing, intimidation, and the threat
of loss of love motivate some renunciation of oedipal
wishes, but she does not develop the same strong superego or give up, really, her infantile genital organization.
Rather, her wishes simply modulate over time.

Though Freud does not say so, one may infer that this
gradual giving up in disappointment of oedipal wishes
could account for the lesser insistence of female libidinal
drives in comparison with male. The notable lack of active female sexual desire in "normal" femininity would
then result from a sort of postoedipal atrophy. Indeed,
female desire in this model remains only for the missing
organ, the penis, rather than for the sexual object—the
father, or men more generally. The girl's sexual desire
here is thus quickly transferred to the desire for a baby
from her father, a baby symbolizing the penis, and therefore preferably a boy baby who brings the missing penis
with him. Freud thus draws upon penis envy and the
penis-baby equation to explain most of what we conventionally mean, and what he explicitly means, by femininity: the girl achieves heterosexuality as she turns to
her father to get a penis (= child); she gains maternality,
the desire for a child (= penis), as a byproduct of penis
envy.

The centrality of penis envy to this account cannot be
overstressed. Freud contrasts the girl's reaction to the
genital difference between the sexes with that of the
boy. The boy's first reaction is denial or disavowal; he
sees nothing. (In other writings, Freud describes how

this reaction carries over into male fetishism: the grown man attempts to fantasize a female phallus and deny the threat of his own castration.) In the normal case, he gradually accepts the evidence of his senses, as the threat of castration terrorizes him into believing that he too could be penisless and that there really are penisless creatures in the human world. For Freud, the boy's earliest sexual interests and curiosity may concern either the genital difference between the sexes or the riddle of where babies come from.

The girl, by contrast, "behaves differently. She makes her judgement and her decision in a flash. She has seen it and knows that she is without it and wants to have it. . . . she develops, like a scar, a sense of inferiority." Both sexes develop contempt for women. The boy feels "horror of the mutilated creature or triumphant contempt for her," and the girl "begins to share the contempt felt by men for a sex which is the lesser in so important a respect." The girl gives up her clitoral masturbation, a painful reminder of her castrated state, and eventually, during puberty, instigates in herself a "wave of repression" that replaces her "masculine" sexuality with femininity.[8] In the unsuccessful case she continually struggles with compulsive, renewed autoerotic demands throughout puberty and into her adult analysis. Unlike the boy's, the girl's first sexual interests always concern the question of genital difference rather than the question of where babies come from.

Freud returns to these themes in "Analysis Terminable and Interminable." Here, he suggests that the desperate female wish for a penis both generates the "strongest motive in coming for [psychoanalytic] treatment" and constitutes biological "bedrock," a final, unanalyzable resistance to psychoanalysis. Men's struggle against passive submission to men, signifying castration, has an equivalent bedrock position. Both stances center on the "repudiation of femininity" and the meaning of the penis.[9]

In "Some Psychical Consequences," Freud begins to query the "prehistory" of the Oedipus complex—the conditions in both sexes that lead to its emergence—but it is in his 1931 "Female Sexuality" that this query is more fully developed. Freud indicates in all three papers, as well as in the lecture "Femininity," that he is writing under pressure. He refers implicitly to his recent cancer operations and his fear of death, and he discusses explicitly the challenges of feminists, other writers in the field eager to seize on half-truths (presumably, to publish before him), the challenges to his position by Karen Horney, Melanie Klein, and Ernest Jones, and the welcome contributions of women analysts who share his perspective.

The work of female analytic colleagues especially instigates "Female Sexuality," which extensively revaluates and discusses the preoedipal mother-daughter relationship that precedes and leads up to the girl's penis envy and her turn to her father. Freud still believes that castration is centrally important to female psychology, but in this work castration is not the center of investigation. He acknowledges that the clinical work of female analysts—he singles out Jeanne Lampl-de Groot and Helene Deutsch and mentions in passing Ruth Mack Brunswick—has led him to recognize an intense, long-lived, exclusive, passionate preoedipal attachment characterized by phallic (active, clitoral) desires.[10] In his reformulation, the father suddenly declines in libidinal significance: the girl sees him now as "not much else . . . than a troublesome rival," and the puzzling question of why she ever gives up her attachment to her mother emerges. Freud concludes, in fact, that the Oedipus complex is never so absolute in the girl as in the boy: "It is only in the male child that we find the fateful combination of love for the one parent and simultaneous hatred for the other as a rival."[11] Attachment to the mother is in many cases never given up completely, and many women carry over the character of their attachment to their mothers to their attachments to their fathers and husbands.

One reading of the female Oedipus complex here would privilege Persephone, torn from and always maintaining her attachment to her mother, Demeter.[12] Such a reading is certainly supported by the 1931 and 1933 accounts, as well as by the Lampl-de Groot and Deutsch accounts that Freud draws upon and by later psychoanalytic writings. But Freud also stresses the number of grievances the girl comes to have toward her mother—the turning of love into hostility. The mother does not and cannot reciprocate the intensive exclusivity of childhood love with its totalistic but unspecified demands for satisfaction; she does not seem to feed sufficiently, has other children, arouses and then forbids sexual activity, and, finally, is responsible for not providing her daughter with a penis. Freud puzzles over the different fate of the daughter's and the son's attachment, sometimes according most weight to the fact that only the daughter has received the extra blow of no penis, sometimes allowing that all such intense love—presumably the boy's as well, insofar as he is not terrorized out of it by the threat of castration—is doomed to perish simply because it is so intense.

Freud here gives us that picture of the development of "normal femininity" that has gone into the psychoanalytic and cultural lexicon as *the* psychology of woman. But "normal" here has become conflated with normative—the development of femininity as a particular psychological organization in some women, within an empirical description of various pathways (albeit some regarded as normal and desirable, others as pathological or deviant) that different women follow, becomes female development in general—and so it has progressed in later psychoanalytic writing.

Thus, even this seemingly monolithic account describes several possible outcomes to women's sexual development. The "normal," desirable outcome is "femininity," but Freud stresses two "nonfeminine" outcomes in female development as well. In one, there is a general sexual inhibition or revulsion against sexuality, as the girl gives up (or, in clitoral masturbation, struggles with) her phallic sexuality along with her masculine identities. In the second, she "cling[s] with defiant self-assertiveness to her threatened masculinity."[13] This problematic masculine outcome foregrounds a girl who, when she must give up her father, identifies with him instead. In both cases the girl gives up her mother as sexual object and object of attachment without turning to her father as a sexual object; in the latter case, she turns to him as an object of identification. Freud's account of these two unresolved oedipal outcomes, then, is closer to the model of Athena than of Persephone. This daughter identifies herself totally with her father, does not recognize her mother, and remains object-sexually, if not autoerotically, virginal.

Not only does Freud use clinical material explicitly and implicitly in his reconstructive account of female development and female sexuality; in his cases, clinical fragments, and vignettes women are also empirical, actual, often named, specific subjects in the analytic situation. In this second approach to woman as subject, we have a vivid sense of them and, probably, our own fantasies of what they were like. We think of Dora, Freud's most famous female case, struggling to name her own history and her own psychological and family situation, unheard like Cassandra, bartered and sacrificed by her father like Iphigenia. Dora is the father's and mother's daughter in the worst situation, as she wistfully hopes for love and affection from a mother and a mother substitute who is in reality her father's lover. Consciously, she denies sexual desire—or expresses it symptomatically; unconsciously, she is primarily homosexually attached at the developmental level of an adolescent crush that conflates the desire for merger and caretaking with sexual desire. She is rejected by Freud, who treats her as an objectively bad, vengeful, fully grown woman rather than as a confused adolescent, and who names her at least partially after a family nursemaid.[14]

Anna O., in actuality Josef Breuer's patient rather than Freud's, is also the father's daughter but a victim of circumstance and her own inner conflicts and desires rather than of conscious manipulation and sacrifice.[15] We suffer with her as she watches over her sick father, as she feels guilty about her fleeting wish to be dancing, as her stiff arm turns into snakes (penis symbols, Freud will later consider them), as she is unable to drink or eat or to speak German or even to speak at all, as various psychically instigated paralyses overtake her, as she daily alternates her lives between two different years. We are relieved at her cure and happy to learn how successfully she later managed her life as active feminist and social worker.

We learn more fleetingly in the *Studies on Hysteria* of Fräulein Elizabeth von R., Frau Emmy von N., and Miss Lucy R., and even less of Katharina, Fräulein Rosalia H., and Frau Cäcilie; of the "Case of Homosexuality in a Woman" and of the many women in the *Introductory Lectures on Psycho-analysis*.[16] Emmy von N., plagued with hysterical conversion symptoms and full of self-recriminations, also manages her large estates and houses, oversees the care and well-being of her two daughters, is an intelligent woman with "an unblemished character and a well-governed mode of life."[17] Frau Cäcilie, whose case is abridged for reasons of confidentiality, suffers from a "violent facial neuralgia," hallucinations, and other hysterical symptoms.[18] Yet she is highly gifted artistically, erudite, and wide-ranging intellectually. Elizabeth von R., like Anna O., is attached to a father whom she then has to nurse through an illness. She feels conflict between sadness at her father's situation and her desire to spend time in the social pleasures of late adolescence, develops hysterical leg pains in relation to the nursing situation, and later becomes guiltily in love with her brother-in-law. Freud suggests to us that nursing the sick—a woman's responsibility—often plays a role in the genesis of hysteria: the nurse's fatigue combines with the need to suppress all emotion, and enforced immobility can lead to flourishing fantasy development. Miss Lucy R., a governess, suffers like Elizabeth von R. from conflicts between erotic desires and feelings of rejection by, in this case, her employer. Katharina's trauma is more direct; she has almost been an incest victim and has witnessed her father's incestuous success with her cousin. Rosalia H. has also suffered from unwanted sexual advances, though not, it seems, rape or seduction.

In all these accounts we see Freud beginning to understand the implication of sexual desire (in the cases of Anna O., Elizabeth von R., and Lucy R. most explicitly) and sexual trauma (an explicit event in the cases of Katharina and Rosalia H., trauma as conflict in the other three) in the genesis of hysteria; with him, we first see them in the actual lives of individual women. Sexuality is a factor also in cases of unnamed women: the desire of the patient in a "case of homosexuality" for a "society lady" of bad reputation and questionable sexual propriety, partly in reaction to feelings toward her father; sexual shame, as far as we can make this out, in the vignette of the married woman whose obsessive symptom consisted in running into a room and calling her maid to a position where the maid could see a stain on a tablecloth, symbolizing in reverse the stain that was not on the wedding sheets when her newly wedded husband was impotent; the obsessive arranging of bedclothes and pillow that symbolized a girl's separation of mother and father and substitution of herself for one or the other in the parental bed.[19]

In a research study, when I interviewed many women members of the second generation of analysts—those trained in the 1920s and 1930s—several claimed that one attraction to the field was that Freud saw women as sexual subjects rather than objects.[20] In the *Studies on Hysteria* and other clinical vignettes we catch some glimpse of this sexual subjectivity, which, as I have indicated, is not present in Freud's account of theoretical woman as subject.[21] I do not suggest that women in these cases are sexual free spirits; they are for the most part afflicted with the physical and mental pain of hysterical symptoms or the overriding insistence of obsessional neurosis. But their sexuality is clearly neither feminine-passive—without lust—nor, with the exception of the "case of homosexuality," masculine (following Freud's definition of masculinity in women). Inhibition and frigidity characterize neurosis for Freud, but the conflicted sexuality described in some of these cases does not fit the closer-to-asexual model that he later describes.

In a third approach, considering woman as subject-object, or object to a self that constructs and reconstructs her subjectivity, we are led to examine further the mother-daughter relationship and its meanings for the daughter. Within Freud's work we cannot see the relationship from the mother's point of view. Possibly because of the centrality of the genetic and reconstructive approaches in psychoanalysis—in which the focus is on the developing child as this development occurs or is (re)constructed—or possibly, it might be argued, because of his real inability to identify with mothers, Freud's writings show a striking lack of interest in the parenting relationship from the perspective of the parent, and especially of the mother. (The father does, after all, threaten to castrate his son, whereas the mother simply sits passively as her imagined sexuality goes from phallic to castrated and as she is and is not an object of attachment or sexual desire to son or daughter. At most, she "seduces" the child and awakens his or her sexuality through early caretaking ministrations.) We do learn of Frau Emmy von N.'s concerns about her daughters, as well as the concerns of Anna O.'s mother and the parents of Fräulein Elizabeth von R. The mother-daughter relationship for the most part, however, is a relationship seen from the point of view of the daughter.[22]

There is a unique complexity of identificatory and object-relational experiences and tasks for the daughter as she sorts out this relation to her mother. Clinically, Freud describes for us Dora's attachment to her mother and to Frau K.; he also describes that of the girl who is the subject of his paper on female homosexuality. He tells us that all children originally experience the importance of the breast as first object and of early maternal care. Freud's late theory, following especially Lampl-de Groot, argues that the girl remains in the negative oedipal position—attached to her mother—for a long time. She may never give up this attachment completely, and she certainly does not dissolve her Oedipus complex as absolutely as does the boy.

Even as he describes this long period of attachment, however, Freud also describes the girl strongly and forcefully turning on her mother—this mother who denied her milk, love, and the phallus. In the daughter's view during this period in her development the mother has withheld what she could have chosen to give. The daughter tries to resolve her situation. At first, all children think everyone is anatomically constructed like them. When the girl then learns that some people have penises but she does not, she assumes that her mother does and that she herself will have one when she grows up. She then realizes that she will never have one and (Freud is unclear here) believes either that her mother has chosen never to give one to her and hasn't got one herself, or that, although she doesn't have one, she could have arranged things so that

her daughter did. In any case, there is great disappointment and a radical distancing from her mother. The
daughter, like the son, introjects an image of mother
and breast as object; in the daughter's psyche, mother
becomes an ambivalently loved and hated object.

But the oedipal resolution, as Freud describes it (generically, it seems, though possibly he speaks only of the
boy), involves an identification with the same-sex parent through which the ego itself is transformed. The
girl, then, must identify with this same mother, who is
an ambivalent, narcissistic (an object like the self) object of attachment, in order to attain her "normal femininity"; the mother must be taken in as subject as well
as object. But what should be the ego ideal—the maternal object-become-subject that is taken in as "normal
femininity"—is a castrated, denying subject. This castrated, denying subject becomes, as a result of identificatory processes, part of the self of the girl even as the
mother-as-object remains, interpersonally and intrapsychically, an object of ambivalent love and hate. Freud
does not extend his discussion of the girl's psychological
dilemma as her identification with her mother supposedly proceeds, but there are clear implications: for
the further reinforcement of the girl's sense of inferiority (no longer a matter just of penis envy but also of
identification with a debased oedipal object); for the
problematic path to maternality (a path that bypasses
identification with the mother); and, as I suggest in the
next chapter, for the construction of an asymmetrical
heterosexuality.

When we think of Freud's writings on women as subjects, we generally mean the developmental account of
theoretical woman or, occasionally, the richly textured
descriptions of clinical women. In both kinds of accounts, but especially in the latter, we can also find the
fourth and fifth approaches to women as subjects: wom-

en as social-historical subjects, and women as contributors to psychoanalysis.

Freud as psychoanalyst is most interested in the inner
psychic worlds, self-constructions, and conflicts of wom-
en. He is also a man of his time, however, and—especially
in those writings that precede his mid-1920s discussions
of female sexuality—one who expresses firm opinions
about the social situation of women and sexuality. I have
mentioned Freud's linking of sickbed-nursing with hysteria. He is also firm in his strong defense of the morality
and upstanding qualities and capabilities of the hysterical women whom contemporary neurologists and psy-
chiatrists considered morally degenerate, mentally con-
taminated, and inferior as a result of their heredity.[23]

In his early discourse "'Civilized' Sexual Morality and
Modern Nervousness," Freud mounts a powerful critique
of the societally, culturally, and familially induced constraint on women's (and men's) sexuality and of the trap
that marriage becomes for many women.[24] These women,
raised in restrictive sexual environments and held close
to their families, are suddenly thrust into marriages with
men who have themselves been constrained and whose
sexuality has been autoerotic or engaged with debased
objects (on this, more below)—men who are thus, for
their own reasons, unlikely to make sympathetic initial
sexual and marriage partners for properly brought-up
women. Freud implies that female neurosis may result
from or be facilitated by this marital situation (since all
neurotic symptoms and character in general result in his
view from both inner, early developmental and constitutional factors *and* from external factors in the person's
current situation), as neurotic symptomatology enables
withdrawal from a difficult situation and expresses anger at the same time. He points to the problematic situation of upper-middle-class women in a vignette that he
labels "In the Basement and on the First Floor" (what we

might now call "Upstairs, Downstairs"). He describes two girls of different classes who engage in childhood sex play, the lower-class girl as part of her path toward a normal and healthy heterosexuality, the upper-class girl— racked by guilt and educated in ideals of feminine purity and abstinence—as prelude toward sexual inhibition and neurosis.[25]

Freud's defense of homosexuality parallels his defense of hysteria. In the *Three Essays on the Theory of Sexuality,* and later in "The Psychogenesis of a Case of Homosexuality in a Woman," he argues that homosexual object choice is on a continuum with heterosexuality ("one must remember that normal sexuality too depends upon a restriction in the choice of object"); that everyone is bisexual ("in all of us, throughout life, the libido normally oscillates between male and female objects"); that homosexuality does not necessarily have to do with physical abnormality, since people of all sexual orientations may show secondary sex characteristics of the other sex; and that many homosexuals are morally and intellectually outstanding. Specifically, his own lesbian patient is a "beautiful and clever girl of eighteen, belonging to a family of good standing" and "not in any way ill."[26] The story of her development to homosexual object choice via jealousy of her mother's pregnancy, desire for a baby from her father, and anger at him for not providing one is an unremarkable story of oedipal development. The girl's intense attachment to her mother presages Freud's 1931 change in theoretical emphasis.

Freud differentiates here, more clearly than in any other part of his writing, between gender identity ("the sexual characteristics and sexual attitude of the subject") and object choice, arguing that either a "masculine" or a "feminine" woman might love women. Moreover, he is somewhat taken aback and somewhat amused by the willfulness and independence of his patient, including (he responds here much more generously and flexibly than in the case of Dora) her attempts to deceive him and to thwart the analysis. He describes her as "a spirited girl, always ready for romping and fighting" and a "feminist [who] felt it to be unjust that girls should not enjoy the same freedom as boys," even as he emphasizes her penis envy.[27] Freud is sympathetic toward her parents, but he seems, really, to agree with their condemnation of their daughter's object choice and their desire to change it only to the extent that he believes that she has (partly out of a motive of revenge) picked as her love object a person of dubious morals and behavior. Moral character, rather than gender, makes this love object unsuitable.

Women are subjects not only of their psychological development, clinical experience, or social and cultural location. As patients and analysts, Freud's writings make clear, women have helped to develop psychoanalytic theory and technique, and he is often generous with his acknowledgment of these contributions. Anna O.'s "chimney-sweeping" created the talking cure. Emmy von N.'s complaints about Freud's interrupting her associations and Elizabeth von R.'s inability to respond to hypnosis led to the method of free association. Hysterical women taught him the varieties of symptom formation: Frau Cäcilie showed how symbolic word associations could be transformed: a grandmother's "piercing" look could lead to pain in the forehead; feeling "stabbed in the heart," to chest pain; an insult, or "slap in the face," to facial neuralgia.[28] Tracking down the source of Miss Lucy R.'s aversion to cigar smoke and burnt pudding and Anna O.'s inability to drink water helped create the trauma theory of symptom formation and the technical practice (no longer rigidly employed) of working back step by step to the origin of each symptom.

Women helped create and make visible transference and countertransference. Freud sees clearly Anna O.'s

eroticized transference to Breuer and even Breuer's countertransference, though he has a name for the latter only
much later, and he takes the transference of woman patient to male doctor to be paradigmatic and emblematic
of transference in general.[29] Women also created or inspired those transferences that were invisible to Freud.
He does not link Miss Lucy R.'s preoccupations with cigar
smoke to his own smoking. Notoriously, he does not see
his own virulent negative countertransference to Dora or
his wistful, fatherly, hovering transference to Elizabeth
von R., in whose future he interested himself to the extent
of procuring an invitation to a ball to which she was invited and acknowledging, ruefully, that "since then, by
her own inclination, she has married someone unknown
to me."[30]

   Women as analysts were also direct contributors to
Freud's understandings of women and to other aspects
of psychoanalytic theory and technique as well. Discussion of this topic is beyond the scope of this chapter except to note some confusions, addressed more fully below, concerning the extent to which women analysts
made these contributions as colleagues or, in direct and
indirect ways, as patients, of Freud's.

When we think about Freud on women, we do not typically refer to the five approaches to woman as subject
that I have delineated, but to Freud's conceptualization
of female development or female sexuality—what I consider as theoretical woman in the developmental theory.
We can also situate and relativize this explicit theoretical treatment of woman as subject in another way, in
relation not to other accounts of woman as subject but
to accounts of woman as object. I believe that Freud's
writings offer a strong, consistent treatment of what we
might consider to be woman in the male psyche: that is,
woman as object, not subject.
   Such a claim is in some ways self-evident: Freud was,

after all, a man, and any account of women that he produced is, finally, an account of women viewed through
the mind of a man. But I mean, rather, that Freud gave
us, both explicitly and implicitly, psychodynamic accounts of how men view women (or certain women) as
objects or others, and of what femininity and women
mean in the masculine psyche. There is something intu-
itively more convincing in these accounts of woman as
object in the male psyche than in those of woman as
subject; indeed, they do not seem to have been widely
criticized (for their accuracy as portrayals, in any case)
in the psychoanalytic or feminist literature since Freud.
The way that both male and female writers seem more
or less to agree with and elaborate upon Freud's claims
in this area—claims, for example, about male fetishism,
masculine fear or contempt of women, and problems in
men's heterosexual object choice and experience—is in
striking contrast to the way that female writers especially, but also some male writers, have taken issue with
almost everything Freud claims about women as subjects. I will return to the question of whether his view of
woman as subject may also be a picture of woman's experience as seen or imagined by man, but that is not my
concern in this discussion.

In examining Freud's explicit treatments of women
as objects, one must acknowledge Karen Horney, who
covers in her discussions of "The Flight from Womanhood" and "The Dread of Woman" most of what needs
to be said on the subject of men's fear and contempt of
women; and Melanie Klein, who in her early writings
on the Oedipus complex also unpacks for us the prehistory of men's (and women's) fear and contempt of wom-
en and flight from femininity.[31] Insofar as Freud's discussions of male development and masculinity center
on the masculine castration complex, it can be said that
he is preoccupied, indeed obsessed, with the meaning in
the male psyche of the female, of sexual difference, and

of what marks this difference. Presence of the penis distinguishes the male, and "Nature has, as a precaution,
attached . . . a portion of his narcissism to that particular organ."[32]

Freud discusses women as sex objects to men in "A
Special Type of Choice of Object Made by Men" and "On
the Universal Tendency to Debasement in the Sphere of
Love" (in which his developmental account implies that
this "universal" tendency is found exclusively in the
male).[33] Men, he suggests, split women symbolically
and erotically into mothers, or mothers and sisters, on
the one hand, and prostitutes on the other. The former
cannot be sexually desired, though they are supposed
to be the kind of woman a man should marry; the latter, though they are maritally and socially forbidden,
can be sexually desired. As long as a woman symbolizes the mother, she is a forbidden oedipal object, an
indication of an attachment carried on too long. Fleeing
to a woman who is or is like a prostitute protects the
defensively constructed idea of the mother's sexual purity and denies oedipal desire. Alternatively, it equates
the mother with a prostitute, thereby giving her son access to her along with his father. Psychically derived impotence follows the same line of reasoning: men become
impotent with women who are like, or who represent
psychically, their mothers. Freud here gives us the psychodynamics of a split long present in Western culture,
literature, and social organization. Indeed, the wife
must eventually reciprocate her husband's setting her
up as an asexual mother, for "a marriage is not made
secure until the wife has succeeded in making her husband her child as well and in acting as a mother to
him."[34]

Some men do not stop with the simple expedient of
separating sexual from asexual women; they must deny
the female sexual constitution altogether. "Fetishism,"
claims Freud, is "a substitute . . . for a particular and

quite special penis": that is, the penis that the mother was once thought to have.[35] All boys struggle with acknowledging females'—originally the mother's—castration. Fetishists resolve the struggle by disavowal or denial, creating a fetish that externally represents the maternal phallus and thus supports such disavowal.

Disavowal also enters the realm of mythology. Medusa's snakes condense signification on the one hand of the mature female external genitals and on the other of many penises, which in turn stand both for castration (because the one penis has been lost) and denial of castration (because there are many penises). Medusa's decapitated head, the castrated female genitals, evokes horror and even paralysis—a reminder of castration—in the man who looks at it, but this paralysis is also an erection, thereby asserting that the penis is still there. In this two-page vignette Freud captures the extreme horror at castration and at the fantasied potential destructiveness of women and the female genitals, which in other writings he glosses with milder words such as "contempt."[36]

The phallic mother is also important in female development; the girl, when she first learns about sexual difference, believes that her mother has a penis and that she will too when she grows up. For both sexes, the preoedipal mother is in Freud's view "phallic": that is, active. But the recognition of the mother's castration seems more permanently traumatic to the boy: "No male human being is spared the fright of castration at the sight of the female genital."[37] The girl is, finally, much more traumatized by a castration of her own. In Freud's view, a more drastic solution than fetishism to conflict over the mother's castration (fetishism, after all, still enables a heterosexual object choice with fetish added on as phallus) is homosexuality, in which the partner himself possesses the phallus directly.[38]

Like theoretical women and femininity itself, clinical

women are presented as objects as well as subjects in Freud's writings. In the "Irma" dream several doctors inject, palpate, minutely examine, and try to cure Irma, who recalcitrantly and vindictively tries to undermine their efforts.[39] Servant women—Grusha, seen from behind as she bends over scrubbing the floor; the governesses Fräulein Peter and Fräulein Lina allowing their small charge to play with their genitals; and Lina, squeezing abscesses from her buttocks at night—play important roles in the formation of neurotic symptomatology in both the Wolf Man and the Rat Man and specify clinically and developmentally the class splits described in the "Contributions to the Psychology of Love."[40] Class here intertwines with gender and sexuality in the formation of male erotic desire.

Freud's perspective from within the male psyche toward both abstract woman and individual clinical women as object, and his ease of identification with men in this stance, produce what has seemed to many commentators a notable amorality in his views of male behavior. I am referring not so much to his giving up of the seduction hypothesis (it seems clear that Freud made his about-face for theoretical and social as well as evidential reasons, but that he was certainly at the same time well aware of the prevalence and negative impact of the sexual abuse of children and of incest) as I am to particular clinical cases. Freud barely notes that Dora's father gave her mother syphilis and that his illness may have affected his children's health as well. He condemns neither this father, who handed Dora over at the age of fourteen to a grown man, nor Herr K., who was willing to accept the gift and who tried to seduce her. The case of Paul Lorenz, the Rat Man, is presented with objectivity muted by empathy, and it is a masterful rendition of the phenomenology of obsessive neurosis. But Freud mentions only in passing, as interesting fact, that Lorenz may have seduced his sister and that he certainly felt free to seduce and use a

range of other women—sometimes with drastic consequences, as he apparently drove one of them to suicide. In
the case vignette of the "dear old uncle" who had the hab-
it of taking the young daughters of friends for outings, arranging for their being stranded overnight, and mastur-
bating them, Freud remarks only on the man's creation of
symbolic equivalence between clean or dirty money and
clean or dirty hands, and he queries the possible health
consequences to the girls of the man's hands being dirty.
But he does not even note, let alone comment forcefully
on, the man's hands being used to masturbate the young
daughters of friends in the first place.[41]

Freud's account of the male psyche represents women,
and especially the mother, not only explicitly but implicitly, or latently, as object. In *Civilization and Its Discontents* he contrasts the "oceanic feeling" with longing for
the father as the origin of religious feeling. This oceanic
feeling—resonant with "limitless narcissism" and in contrast to which mature ego-feeling in later life seems a
"shrunken residue"—is very clearly, though not stated as
such, the original feeling of the infant with its mother. It
is not longing for the mother, for lost narcissistic oneness,
then, that generates religious need but longing for the father. This longing results from "infantile helplessness" in
the face of fear.[42] As the account develops, it becomes clear
that the fear Freud refers to is oedipal fear and fear of castration: precisely, the boy's fear of his father, merged with
his love for him. What begins here as an impersonal oceanic feeling, held by generic human beings of both sexes,
turns out to be contrasted with a specifically masculine
relation to the father, which Freud thus sees emphatically
as more important for the boy than the relation to the
mother.

Even less explicitly acknowledged than the mother
who signifies the limitless narcissism of childhood is
the idealized mother, symbolized by her breast and her
sometimes perfect love. In striking contrast to the deval-

uation and contempt for the mother that he displays elsewhere and to his minimizing of the importance of this early relation in *Civilization and Its Discontents*, Freud also claims that "sucking at the mother's breast is the starting-point of the whole of sexual life, the unmatched prototype of every later sexual satisfaction. . . . I can give you no idea of the important bearing of this first object upon the choice of every later object, of the profound effects it has in its transformations and substitutions in even the remotest regions of our sexual life."[43] Such sucking is ostensibly gender-free, but Freud later implies that the satisfaction and its sequelae may be gender-differentiated. It is hard to separate male wish-fulfillment from objective description of the female psyche when Freud tells us that "a mother is only brought unlimited satisfaction by her relation to a son; this is altogether the most perfect, the most free from ambivalence of all human relationships."[44]

In Freud's Pantheon, then, masculine images of the mother seem to oscillate between an Aphrodite—all mature heterosexual love and global eroticized giving, perhaps with a touch of narcissism, in love with her son and his penis—and someone who, like Hera, is more vengeful, strong and insistent, resentful of men and their betrayals. Not only is this latter mother herself castrated, but she castrates, or threatens to castrate, both her son and her daughter. In contrast to Jungian writing, Demeter—the mother who loves the daughter and mourns her loss—is nowhere to be found.[45]

In "The Taboo of Virginity" Freud suggests that women other than mothers—specifically, recently deflowered ex-virgins—might castrate a man or take his penis in revenge for their painful defloration.[46] In many cultures, therefore, the custom is *jus primae noctis*: the right of strong, powerful, older men to perform a bride's defloration. Having discussed at length elsewhere the girl's penis envy as well as her very problematic sexual socialization,

Freud here suggests in passing that a virgin may indeed be hurt or resent her first experience of intercourse; a husband, who must live with his wife for some time, should be spared her revenge and anger. To build our sense of horror, Freud invokes the decapitating (castrating) Judith and Holofernes, but he is much more certain of the part male fantasy plays in the custom: "Whenever primitive man has set up a taboo he fears some danger and it cannot be disputed that a generalized dread of women is expressed in all these rules of avoidance. The man is afraid of being weakened by the woman, infected with her femininity. . . . The effect which coitus has of discharging tensions and causing flaccidity may be the prototype of what the man fears."[47] Even worse, it seems, than the impotence and lack of sexual desire that Freud suggests in the first two "Contributions to the Psychology of Love," is the possibility of total weakening and "infection" with femininity. The young, innocent husband must be protected against such a psychic threat. We must ask, in this context, if the imagined reaction of the girl is not almost entirely that of a man imagining how he would feel if reminded by intercourse of his lack of a penis.

Freud presents as objective truth a final version of woman as subject that is, like the resentment of defloration, really an extension of imaginings and beliefs held by the male psyche. He describes a variety of traits that characterize a woman and that he attributes entirely to penis envy and women's lack of a penis. These include shame about her body, jealousy (arising directly from the envy itself), a lesser sense of justice (resulting from the weak female superego, a superego that never fully forms because the girl does not fear castration and does not therefore give up oedipal longings or internalize sexual prohibitions), and narcissism and vanity as the self-love that a man centers on his penis becomes defensively diffused throughout the female body. As Freud acknowledges, feminists in his time accused him of male bias in these views. He also points out—in possible contradiction to his resting his case on clinical findings—that these are "character-traits which critics of every epoch have brought up against women."[48] As cultural man, then, he seems to have borrowed a variety of masculine cultural attitudes toward women, whose origins he then coincidentally attributes to the process of female development.

We are thus led back to our place of beginning, the theory of femininity. At various points Freud claims that active and passive are our best approximations of masculine and feminine, but he in fact focuses much more on the distinction between phallicly endowed and castrated: women, basically, are castrated men. I am not the first person to ask where his overwhelming preoccupation with the penis and castration —male organs and a threat to masculine body integrity, as Freud himself, along with later psychoanalytic commentators, verifies—comes from. We have good reason, from his own account, to think that such a preoccupation comes from the boy; that as Freud wonders about femininity, he is asking, as one commentator puts it, "What is femininity—*for men?*"[49] I have tried to sort out his approach to women as subjects, women as objects to their own subjectivity, and women as explicit and implicit objects in the male psyche. But we are left with this problem: what part of the Freudian construction of woman as subject is really constructed after the fact from the central conflict and trauma in Freud's theory of sexuality, based on an explicit and implicit male norm? Is he asking, as Horney suggests, how a man or boy would feel if he were someone without a penis?[50] Hence, woman as manifest subject becomes, possibly, a latent projection of man.

Freud claims, quite rightly, that his theory comes from clinical experience, and he supports it by drawing upon the writings of several women analysts. But the issue of clinical experience in early psychoanalysis is complicated. For one thing, the women analysts he cites—Deutsch, Lampl-de Groot, and Brunswick—were themselves analyzed by Freud, as was Marie Bonaparte, whose later theorizing on the connections of femininity, masochism, and passivity became Freudian orthodoxy on the psychology of women.[51] Like other analysands, these women analysts seem to have remained trans-ferentially and in actuality attached. Lampl-de Groot, even as she provides the basis for a radically new theory, does not take issue with Freud's claim for the centrality of the female castration complex. Indeed, she reviews almost everything he has written before suggesting—modestly, on the basis of two cases—that there might possibly be something he left out. Deutsch and Anna Freud in their own writings give evidence that they wanted to please Freud by the kinds of theories they cre-ated, and they have more than once been taken to task on this account.

Moreover, as the biographical literature on psychoan-alysts expands, we are becoming more aware of just how autobiographical the early writings often were. These first analysts, after all, did not have a lot of cases, and one knows—even as one doesn't know—oneself best. Freud makes it quite explicit that his theory of the Oedipus complex evolved from his own self-analysis. His *Inter-pretation of Dreams* stands as a classic account of psycho-analytic theory creation through self-analysis. We do not know about other occasions when he may have used him-self as a case without acknowledging the fact. Other writ-ings are not so candid. A biography of Deutsch and her own autobiography make clear the autobiographical ba-sis, translated into fictive case accounts, of much of her theory of femininity, and among early women writers on women Deutsch is a leading defender and supporter of the theories of primary penis envy, narcissism, maso-

chism and passivity. Elizabeth Young-Bruehl suggests
that Freud's "Dissolution of the Oedipus Complex" and
"Some Psychical Consequences of the Anatomical Distinction between the Sexes," as well as the earlier paper
"A Child Is Being Beaten," come at least partially (and
probably entirely in "A Child") from his analysis of his
daughter Anna, whose own writings on beating fantasies and on altruism are themselves autobiographical
though presented fictively as cases. Both Deutsch and
Anna Freud, in writings now available, affirm at some
length their hatred and jealousy of mothers, who are all
bad, and their idealization of fathers, who are virtually
all good.[52]

Freud's "clinical experience" with women patients,
then, from the end of World War I through the mid-
1920s—just before his writings on femininity—involved
those same women who wrote of themselves and of their
own patients as they supported and helped to create his
position. Did, and how did, his analysis of these young
women followers—including Anna, the one nearest and
dearest to him—affect his theory? How much were the
autobiographical and theoretical understandings reflected in their writings on femininity affected by their
analysis with Freud—a Freud who, as we know from his
classic case reports, was not loath to offer his patients
interpretations based on previously conceived theories?
These understandings, translated by at least Deutsch
and Anna Freud into fictive patient accounts as well as
into theory, must have emerged at least partially from
interpretations and reconstructions made by that very
powerful and charismatic person who later used *their*
writings as independent corroboration of his own position. They may well have been reflecting their own
experience—there are certainly women with the particular configuration of love and hate for father and mother they describe, and women who for a variety of reasons express envy of or desire for a penis, or passive or

masochistic sexual desires—but they cast their writings in universal terms, as characterizing femininity per se. And Freud, for theoretical reasons, used them that way as well.

The problem here is not the partially autobiographical basis of these early psychoanalytic writings. Though it is only recently that, under the name of countertransference, analysts have been publicly willing to open themselves as extensively to scrutiny, much early psychoanalytic theory (I do not speculate about psychoanalytic theory today) was autobiographically based, and in the case of the theory of femininity, as elsewhere, the opposition (Horney and Klein, for instance) almost certainly drew upon implicit autobiographical understandings as well.[53] I want to direct attention to the special complexities in the case of Freud's views on the psychology of women and the somewhat less than independently developed clinical and theoretical support he draws upon. We can only begin to untangle the convoluted interactions in theory creation here, but we are certainly thereby invited to rethink such theory.

Although Freud claimed that his understanding of women was "incomplete and fragmentary" and that the girl's attachment to her mother seemed "grey with age and shadowy,"[54] he nevertheless developed a broad-sweeping theory about femininity and treated and discussed many women clinically. For the most part we admire his clinical accounts, his forthright defense of hysterical women, and his condemnation of the conditions leading to repression and hysteria in women. We admire also his toleration and understanding of variations in sexual object choice and sexual subjectivity. Yet though we are still not able completely to evaluate his theory of femininity, most evaluations find it extremely problematic.

By contrast, Freud's understandings about male attitudes toward women and femininity do not seem at all fragmentary and incomplete. They are specific, informative, persuasive, precise; they cover, ingeniously, a variety of sexual, representational, and neurotic formations. They illuminate for us, with passion and empathy, masculine fantasies and conflicts. Rethinking Freud on women, then, leaves us with a normative theory of female psychology and sexuality, a rich account of masculinity as it defines itself in relation to women, and several potential openings toward more plural conceptions of gender and sexuality.

2

Heterosexuality As a Compromise Formation

The preceding chapter contrasts the wide variety of Freudian accounts of women (and men) with the account of normal femininity (and masculinity) that we often take to be—and that Freud also takes to be—*the* Freudian theory. This theory of "normal femininity," an account of the normative desiderata of female development, fits itself best into an account of women in heterosexual relationship to men. Along with a complementary account of male development and character, and with Freud's various accounts of perversion and typical masculine object choices, we find in these writings the origins of a psychoanalytic theory of sexuality. Sexuality has always been central to psychoanalysis, and accordingly, there has continued to be since Freud much psychoanalytic attention to sexuality. Yet as we read this literature, we must be struck that it has not much advanced our understanding of heterosexuality.

This chapter unpacks what seem to be psychoanalytic assumptions that take as given a psychosexuality of normal heterosexual development in which deviation from this norm needs explanation but norm-following does not. By "normal" or "ordinary" heterosexuality, I have in mind socially and culturally taken-for-granted assumptions that seem to encompass notions both of the normative and of the statistically prevalent or typical. Within psychoanalysis, normal heterosexuality is represented in Freud's descriptions of the path to normal femininity in girls and the positive oedipal resolution in

boys. We can also define normal heterosexuality negatively, as that which psychoanalysts have tended to see
as *not* requiring special notice, in contrast to homosexuality and the perversions. (To say "normal" does not
imply that there is no variety within heterosexuality or
that such sexuality might not be intensely meaningful
to participants.)

I make two intertwined arguments. First, because
heterosexuality has been assumed, its origins and vi-
cissitudes have not been described: psychoanalysis does
not have a developmental account of "normal" heterosexuality (which is, of course, a wide variety of heterosexualities) that compares in richness and specificity to
accounts we have of the development of the various homosexualities and what are called perversions. Psychoanalytic writers have not paid the kind of attention to heterosexuality that they have to these other identities and
practices; after Freud, most of what one can tease out
about the psychoanalytic theory of "normal" heterosexuality comes by reading between the lines in writings on
perversions and homosexuality.[1]

Second, insofar as we do have a developmental or clinical account of heterosexuality, it seems either to be relatively empty and general or to imply that heterosexuality
is not different in kind from homosexuality, perversion, or
any sexual outcome or practice. Depending upon which
theory is relied on, it is a symptom, a defensive complex, a neurosis, a disorder, a meshing of self-develop-
ment, narcissistic restitutions, object relations, unconscious fantasy, and drive derivatives. Within the theory,
therefore, it is difficult to find persuasive grounds for
distinguishing heterosexuality from homosexuality according to criteria of "health," "maturity," "neurosis,"
"symptom," or any other evaluative terms, or in terms
that contrast "normal" and "abnormal" in other than
the statistical or normative sense. Both are similarly
constructed and experienced compromise formations;

at most, we may be able according to these terms to distinguish perverse from nonperverse within both categories. Since the onus seems to be on homosexuality to prove its nonsymptomatic character, we need to add, moreover, that the almost definitional encoding in heterosexuality of intrapsychic and interpersonal male dominance contributes to its defensive, symptomatic, or restitutive character.

My discussion, of necessity, skirts a problem of connotation in the literature. When this literature refers to homosexuality, homosexuals, homosexual object choice, or a variety of perversions, it seems (apparently reflecting everyday culture) to be referring specifically to sexuality, sexual object choice, fantasy, erotization, or desire—and, in the case of both male homosexuals and lesbians, to someone with a conscious sexual identity.[2] By contrast, accounts of the development or experience of normal heterosexuality seem to mean something more than or "larger than" sex: we are in the realm of "falling in love," "mature love," "romantic passion," "true object love," or "genital love." This love may *include* sexual pleasures and meanings, but it goes beyond them. It is as though heterosexuality is more than a matter of erotic or orgasmic satisfaction, whereas other sexualities are not.[3]

My discussion too addresses only inconsistently the relations between sexuality and gender difference. Given what we know about men and women, their sexuality and its development, there is some question whether we can or should talk generically of either homosexuality or heterosexuality. Nonpsychoanalytic writings on sexuality, as well as contemporary sexual politics, tangle with questions concerning whether "queerness" or gender most defines sexuality, and most psychoanalytic writing tends to differentiate male homosexual from lesbian, focusing on one or the other.[4] Similar considerations would also seem to apply in the heterosexual case. A woman's choice of a male sexual object or lover is typically so different—developmentally, experientially, dynamically, and in its meaning for her womanliness or femininity—from a man's choice of a female sexual object or lover that it is not at all clear whether we should identify these by the same term. We can do so behaviorally and definition- ally—a hetero-object is other than or different from the self, whereas a homo-object is like the self—and there is certainly a culturally normative distinction that con- flates heterosexuals of both genders, but we may thereby confuse our psychological understanding.[5]

In what follows, I focus on specific theorists, but I also consider what I regard as widespread unelabo- rated, paradigmatic accounts and assumptions found in clinical reports, case discussions, theoretical and clini- cal discussions of men or women, and even in articles that do not particularly focus on sexuality or gender. My point is not to condemn or to universalize about psychoanalytic writings but to indicate trends in psy- choanalytic thinking that I think warrant reflection. I suggest a need for more explicit attention to the devel- opment of heterosexuality in both men and women (and imply a need for more explicit attention to the develop- ment of love and passion in homosexuals).

Certain biological assumptions or understandings, I be- lieve, underlie the striking lack of interest in detailed investigation of the developmental genesis of heterosex- uality. The simplest of these—what many psychoana- lysts probably think—is that heterosexuality is innate or natural; it is how humans "naturally" develop as we follow our evolutionary heritage and that of other ani- mal species, especially our primate ancestors. Such a position is regarded as obvious and not in need of de- fense or argument.[6]

There are a number of problems with this kind of psy- choanalytic account. To begin on the level of logical consistency, it implies that we need an explanation for the development of homosexuality or perversion in the individual but that heterosexuality doesn't need explaining. As psychoanalyst Robert Stoller, discussing problems with the assumption of a biologically "natural" heterosexuality, puts it: "Are there really psychoanalysts who believe that human psychic development proceeds 'naturally' with preprogrammed facility?"[7]

A more complex empirical problem with the claim or assumption that people are biologically programmed to be heterosexual is that normal heterosexuality, like all sexual desire, is specified in its object. If it were not, *any* man would suit a heterosexual woman's sexual or relational object need, and vice versa, whereas in fact there is great cultural and individual psychological specificity to sexual object choice, erotic attraction, and fantasy. Any *particular* heterosexual man or woman chooses *particular* objects of desire (or types of objects), and in each case we probably need a cultural and individual developmental story to account for these choices.

By cultural story, I mean the fairytales, myths, tales of love and loss and betrayal, movies, and books that members of a culture grow up with and thus share with others. Since even unconscious fantasy must be constituted at least partially through language, we are not surprised to find that sexual fantasy has partial resonance with these stories, which are individually appropriated in what Ernst Kris has called a "personal myth."[8] As we would expect from this cultural component, notions of sexual attraction and attractiveness vary historically and cross-culturally. In the West, cultural fantasies are almost exclusively heterosexual (Greek myths and tales of male friendship are a notable exception, and of course homosexual love was sanctioned in classic Greek culture, while it has been largely proscribed in ours). In a sense, it is easier to construct heterosexual fantasies because the ingredients are nearer to hand.

Heterosexual fantasy and desire also have an individual component, a private heterosexual erotism that contrasts with or specifies further the cultural norm. To take an everyday example that we all immediately recognize, different ethnicities are likely to have different norms of attractiveness. For both cultural and oedipal reasons (and I do not wish to minimize the influence of hegemonic cultural concepts of attractiveness on these), people who grow up in these ethnicities are likely to build such norms (directly or indirectly, positively or negatively) into their sexual orientation and object choice.[9] Those who are called or who consider themselves heterosexual are, in all likelihood, tall-blond-Wasposexual, short-curly-haired zaftig-Jewishosexual, African-American-with-a-southern-accentosexual, erotically excited only by members of their own ethnic group or only by those outside that group. Some women find themselves repeatedly attracted to men who turn out to be depressed, others to men who are aggressive or violent, still others to narcissists. Some men are attracted to women who are chattery and flirtatious, others to those who are quiet and distant. Some choose lovers or spouses who are like a parent (and it can be either parent for either gender or a mixture of the two); others choose lovers or spouses as much unlike their parents as possible (often to find these mates recapitulating parental characteristics after all, or to find themselves discontented when they don't). These choices have both cultural and individual psychological resonance.

My point is that biology cannot explain the content of either cultural fantasy or private erotism. We need a psychodynamic story to account for the development of any particular person's particular heterosexuality, such that it is difficult to claim that we can draw the line between what needs accounting for and what does not in anyone's sexual development or object choice. Any clinician knows this, but clinicians have tended for pretheoretical reasons to assume that such variety is less important than the overarching division of sexual orientation that our culture has made primary since the nineteenth century.

A final lacuna, or contradiction, in the assumption of innate heterosexuality concerns that assumption's relation to our developmental theories and observations. It contradicts our observations and theory concerning the pansexuality of infants and children and their lack of focus on one zone or mode of gratification, as well as our knowledge that virtually *everyone's* initial bodily erotic involvement is with their mother. We could argue that the mother relation (nursing, body contact, and clinging) is not sexual, but this would be a high price to pay in terms of the psychoanalytic theory of sexuality and the foundational psychoanalytic argument that sexuality is more than genital and reproductive. Moreover, the little evidence we have suggests that gender labeling typically overrides biology in determining sexual orientation, so that for most cases of "mislabeling" or hormonal abnormality, sexual orientation is heterosexual in complementary relation to the labeled gender.[10]

An alternative innatist position—a claim that implicitly refers mainly to male homosexuality—argues that most people are programmed to be heterosexual but that some are programmed homosexual.[11] Psychoanalytic innatist theory is echoed by some nonpsychoanalytic gay theorists. These views, though probably a minority position, respond to how insistent, innate, and unchangeable sexual preference feels. By arguing that sexuality or sexual object choice is biological and insistent, gay theorists challenge claims that homosexuality can be changed (through choice or therapy), or that it is to be morally condemned. If one's sexuality is given, what one is born with, then it is outside the moral (and therapeutic) realm. Gay and lesbian writings seem to diverge here. Against Adrienne Rich's claim that all women would be naturally

lesbian if it were not for "compulsory heterosexuality,"
psychologist Carla Golden reports research demonstrat-
ing that some lesbians see themselves as "primary lesbians"—for whom lesbianism is not a choice but a desire
and sense of "difference" felt from an early age—whereas others see their lesbianism as "elective," consciously
chosen for political or erotic reasons. (Golden does not
address the question of whether primary lesbianism is
biological; what her subjects report is that it develops
early and feels immutable.) [12]

This position raises similar problems to the claim for
universally programmed heterosexuality. It does not allow specificity of object choice beyond homo-, bi-, or
heterosexual; it contradicts the gender-labeling evidence; and it removes the question of sexuality from
psychodynamic concern, since it implies that our developmental stories, transference recapitulations, and understandings about intrapsychic, object-relational, self,
and defensive organization are not so important. Here
too, everyone lives out their biological tendencies, most
of us as heterosexuals.

As clinicians, psychological theorists, or cultural thinkers, then, we are challenged: if everyone's programmed
biology is heterosexual but this goes awry for some who
end up homosexual, then homosexuals have developmental stories but heterosexuals do not. Biology, or evolutionary biology, explains how one kind of sexuality develops
but not other kinds. Even if we want to retain a modified
biological story, like Freud's view that development is a
"complemental series" of interactions between constitution and experience (much of modern biology extends
this view to insist that experience affects biological structure and function as much as the reverse), we must conclude that homosexual and heterosexual development
will have the same *kind* of complemental story: since
each account and each story will be developmentally and

clinically specific, there will be no reason normatively to privilege heterosexuality.

A biological or bioevolutionary explanation of heterosexuality leads us to deny what we know clinically, experientially, culturally, and cross-culturally: that sexual feelings are psychological, charged, and subjectively meaningful and that their particularity can be explained in terms of an individual's psychodynamic life history and cultural-linguistic location. If we accept the biological assumption, we lose our psychology. If we are to retain a psychological approach, recognizing that biology and drives always get embroiled in conflict, fantasy, identity, narcissism, passionate object relating, reparation (the particular psychological theory here is irrelevant), we cannot rely on sexual dimorphism to explain heterosexuality.

By this point in my argument, many readers will quite naturally raise the objection that Freud's view was much more complex, that he never thought heterosexuality was biological. Freud believed that everyone was constitutionally bisexual and that sexual object choice always needed explaining. In the *Three Essays on the Theory of Sexuality* and in "The Psychogenesis of a Case of Homosexuality in a Woman," he protests that there are upstanding homosexuals and that homosexuality is simply one sexuality among many; in "Analysis Terminable and Interminable," he claims that bisexuality is biological and psychological bedrock. The theory of constitutional bisexuality and Freud's clinical cases indeed sustain the view that any sexuality is partly constructed through the repression of its opposite: heterosexual orientation includes repressed homosexuality and vice versa.[13] Freud thought that there were continuities between child and adult sexuality, between homosexuality and heterosexuality, and between normal genitality and perversion.

Yet Freud seems also to have thought (probably for teleological reasons having to do with species reproduction) the opposite—that heterosexuality is natural.[14] At the same time, his own theoretical and clinical accounts of the development of heterosexual orientation in both males and females can be read only as accounts of compromise formations and defense. The boy's terror of castration, based on a fear of and disgust at the female genitals, leads him to give up his mother and fuels his final heterosexual object choice; it is a rare case history that does not recognize castration anxiety and conflict about women in a male patient. A girl's heterosexuality is also fueled by horror at her own genital mutilation, by penis envy, and by rage and hatred toward her mother. Her erotic desire never seems to enter the Freudian picture, as the girl turns to her father not out of libidinal desire but out of narcissistic mortification and a wish to possess his penis as her own organ. When she finds out that she cannot have it, she still does not want him; rather, she wants a baby that will substitute for the penis she cannot have.

There are many inconsistencies here, and Kenneth Lewes's *Psychoanalytic Theory of Male Homosexuality* brilliantly takes apart this classical theory, especially for boys. Lewes points out, for instance, inconsistencies in the account of oedipal identification. Freud tells us in "Mourning and Melancholia" that it is the lost *object* that casts a shadow on the ego; therefore, the boy should identify with his mother, rather than with his father. Prevalent responses to fear (of punishment or castration), by contrast, are anxiety, paralysis, denial, or flight. If the boy identifies with his *father* in resolving his Oedipus complex, it can only be to the extent that the boy's love was homoerotic as well as heteroerotic, to the extent that his *father* was his love object as well as, or rather than, his mother. Lewes also notes Freud's confusion here between behavior and psychology.[15] On the level of *psychological meaning*, the boy's preoedipal love for his mother must be understood as narcissistic and homosexual: the phallic boy (as well as the phallic girl) loves the phallic mother.

Lewes suggests that the origins of normal heterosexuality in the Oedipus complex are much more complicated than Freud and those that follow him believed. He describes twelve different possible oedipal constellations for the boy, depending upon whether his attachment is anaclitic or narcissistic, whether he takes himself or his father or his mother as object, whether this mother is phallic or castrated, whether he identifies with father or (phallic or castrated) mother, and whether his own sexual stance is passive or active. Six of these constellations are heterosexual, but only one—an active sexual stance, employing an anaclitic mode of object choice, taking as object a castrated mother, based on identification with his father—is "normal." Lewes points out that this discovery makes problematic our ability to accord normality to a single sexuality: "the mechanisms of the Oedipus complex are really a series of psychic traumas, and all results of it are neurotic compromise formations. . . . even optimal development is the result of a trauma, [so] the fact that a certain development results from a 'stunting' or 'blocking' or 'inhibition' of another possibility does not distinguish it from other developments. So all results of the Oedipus complex are traumatic, and, for similar reasons, all are 'normal'. . . . the Oedipus complex operates by trauma and necessarily results in neurotic conditions."[16]

I believe that many psychoanalytic theorists have more or less recognized, though they have not forcefully acknowledged, this problem. They do not offer final conclusions on the issue of normality and neurosis. Some, such as Stoller and Ethel Person, describe the "neurotic" core of passion or heterosexuality; others, such as

Joyce McDougall, think that some handlings of the castration "trauma"—while traumatic—are normal and
others not.[17]

Another solution to the Freudian paradox of traumatic
normality seems to involve bypassing or minimizing the
castration complex and seeing the development of heterosexuality in less dynamic, more interpersonal terms.
In what is again a widely assumed though not necessarily
explicitly expressed view that finds its origin in Freud,
the boy is thought to bounce from his natural preoedipal
love for his mother to oedipal love, and then to adult sexual desire for women. Complementarily, the girl's desire
for autonomy from her mother meets with "mild seduction"—a sort of seduction that is not a seduction—by her
father, and she becomes heterosexual.[18]

Although I do not think that the castration complex is
the nodal origin of sexual orientation and desire, it has
virtue as a theoretical center in that it generates consistency in our accounts of all forms of sexual development. Moreover, insofar as Freud's story of the castration complex sees sexuality in developmental, dynamic,
and conflictual terms and recognizes that conscious
and unconscious fantasy go into sexuality, it also accords with our clinical experience.

By comparison, the interpersonal alternative has tre-
mendous problems. To begin, normal heterosexuals in
this account look more or less alike; experientially, their
sexuality does not seem to attain great importance or
meaning for them. This generality and lack of detail
contrast with the fine-tuned specificity and the richness
of psychoanalytic accounts of homosexuality and the
perversions: for example, Freud's, Phyllis Greenacre's,
Janine Chasseguet-Smirgel's, and others' descriptions
of the primitive denials and splits in the ego that enable
a man to deny sexual difference; Stoller's accounts of
the transcending and reversal of humiliation that is at

the core of all perversion; Stoller's and McDougall's descriptions of the driven compulsiveness in perversion;
Robert Stolorow and Frank Lachman's and Charles
Socarides' accounts of self-other problems and gender
identity confusion; or McDougall's, Stoller's and others'
descriptions of extremely problematic maternal and paternal behavior and parental appropriation or punishment of the child's erotism, gender, and pleasure.[19]

The interpersonal account, moreover, does not stand
up to close examination. As Chapter 1 makes clear, psychoanalysts since Freud have repeatedly documented
the defensiveness and fear of women and things feminine that characterize many of the most normal heterosexual men in our society.[20] Male love of and erotic desire for women are not so simple or straightforward.
With the girl's story, we confront a different set of problems: the account glosses over a rather problematic content. Culturally, we might ask, what is the "femininity"
that a father should appreciate in his preschool daughter? Where does it come from? Clinically, we wonder,
why does she engage in what we can only assume are
demure, flirtatious, idealizing behaviors, and why does
she have to do so to win her father's attention? We know
that such behavior is not biologically determined or
even prevalent transhistorically or cross-culturally; it is
historically and culturally specific.

Reciprocally, why do fathers in our society—as many
developmental psychology studies demonstrate—seem
to need to reinforce and instill gender-typed behavior in
their sons and daughters, whereas mothers do not? (Indeed, we take any sexualization of a mother's relationship toward her son to be problematic.)[21] What is appropriate paternal "seductiveness" and heterosexual behavior from father to young daughter, and what do we make
of such a prescriptive model of father-daughter relations
in the context of our growing awareness of the prevalence

of incest, child sexual abuse, and sexual objectification of little girls in our society?

Since Freud, dominant psychoanalytic understandings have moved from some recognition of continuity and commonality among sexualities, and of the problematic nature of everyone's sexuality, to assumptions more in accord with a popular culture that treats only deviant sexualities as problematic. Those few modern psychoanalysts who do discuss heterosexuality (Otto Kernberg, Ethel Person, the German psychoanalyst and ethnographer Fritz Morgenthaler), as well as some of those (McDougall, Stoller, and others) who discuss perversion, point in the directions that I am suggesting.[22] They all give us reason to conclude either that heterosexuality is, like homosexuality and perversion, a defensive structure or compromise formation—in some sense, "symptomatic" or a "disorder"—or that it has symptomatic or defensive features; a few directly address the disorders or problematic features of "normal" sexuality.[23] As Martha Kirkpatrick claims, "Many assertions about homosexuals—hatred of the opposite sex, regression from oedipal disappointments, inability to tolerate the discovery of sexual differences—can be applied equally to many heterosexuals."[24] When we cannot reach such a conclusion, it is in regard to distinguishing elements in heterosexuality that seem to have a *deus ex machina* quality inconsistent with the rest of the account.

Like Freud, post-Freudian theorists tend toward what seems a contradictory position. They claim or imply that homosexuality is less healthy or normal but also indicate that it is not or need not be. Michael Balint, for example, argues for the unique primacy of what he calls (heterosexual) true object love and genitality, and he classes homosexuality as a perversion. At the same time, he asserts that "anybody who has had any experience with homosexuals knows that, in them, we may find practically the whole scale of love and hatred that is exemplified in heterosexuality" and that "one quite often finds in homosexuals an object-love as rich and as diversified as among heterosexuals." Balint classifies homosexuality as a perversion apparently because of what he takes to be "an atmosphere of overpretence and denial" that characterizes perversions more generally: Homosexuals, according to Balint, insist that their sexuality and its pleasures are far superior to those of heterosexuals. They overemphasize "in order to deny— what they all know—that without normal intercourse, there is no real contentment."[25] But it would seem— among psychoanalysts at least—to be heterosexuals who assert the superiority of their own sexuality.[26] Similarly, McDougall refers to "the different homosexualities, some of which do not qualify as neosexualities" (her term for perversions), and she claims that "nondeviant sexuality may also display addictive and compulsive qualities."[27]

Among analysts, Stoller has taken on the issue of normality and neurosis most directly. In some sense putting "perversion" in the center of normal sexuality (Kernberg more recently has taken a similar position),[28] Stoller argues that "the overall structure of erotic excitement . . . is similar in most everyone, [that] it is not [hostile] dynamics that differentiate perversions from the lesser perversions—those states that others call normal or normative behavior—but whether the erotic excitement brings one toward or away from sustained intimacy with another person." His early work according to Stoller, demonstrated that hatred and the desire to humiliate the other, and thereby to revenge oneself and triumph over childhood trauma, formed the basic fantasy script in perversion and pornography. He came subsequently to conclude that "what makes excitement out of boredom for most people is the introducing of hostility into the fantasy." For him, the differentiating criterion in perversion is the "desire to sin . . . to hurt, harm, be cruel to, degrade, *humiliate* someone."[29] But this leads, circularly, back to the conclusion that there is a perverse element in all sexuality, since the desire to sin is itself the hostility that is at the core of sexual excitement for all people.

Stoller indicates a continuum, as he implies a differentiation of what we might consider extremes of perversion and nonperversion without specifying exactly where the dividing line lies. The extent of the desire to harm does allow us to begin to differentiate "perverse" from "nonperverse" sexuality—but it does not do so according to the gender of the object in relation to the self. In both heterosexuality and homosexuality one could "search for the circumstances in which affection, tenderness, and other nonhostile components of love participate in, perhaps even dominate, the excitement." Echoing McDougall, Stoller claims that "it is better to talk of the homosexualities rather than of homosexuality. . . . there are as many different homosexualities as there are heterosexualities."[30]

Person, who writes about love more than sex, takes a similar position. Love between homosexuals, she claims, "is experienced in exactly the same way as it is experienced between heterosexuals. . . . Homosexual love draws fire for much the same reason as adulterous love, it appears to be a threat to the social order. Homosexual love is disapproved of for its unconventionality, its threat to social role, and, perhaps, its threat to people's own security about their sexual identities. However, none of these fears ought to blind others to the experience of the participants themselves, which seems identical to the experience of heterosexuals in love."[31]

The solution to this inconsistent and equivocal treatment would seem to be to see either *both* homosexuality and heterosexuality or *neither* as symptomatic and perverse. Stoller affirms, on the one hand, that "everyone is

erotically aberrant and most people most of the time are
at least a bit perverse" and, on the other, that "homosexuality, like heterosexuality, is a mix of desires, not a
symptom, not a diagnosis."[32] Person (referring implicitly
to heterosexual love) declares: "The customary mental
health prescription for love relies too much on psychic
maturity, but maturity is hardly a guarantor of passion.
Intensity is just as likely to come out of a good neurotic
fit, perhaps with one person needing to be subordinate,
the other dominant."[33]

Among modern writers, Kernberg has most consis-
tently addressed normal heterosexuality, but his writing
seems to oscillate between implying intense, passionate,
sexual love and implying heterosexuality alone. He describes a "continuum of character constellations" in the
capacity to fall and remain in love, at its apogee the "capacity to integrate genitality with tenderness and a stable, mature object relation." Mature love requires not
heterosexual object choice but coming to terms with and
sublimating both homosexual and heterosexual, preoedipal and oedipal, identifications. "Sexual passion is
a basic experience of simultaneous forms of transcendence beyond the boundaries of the self. [It] reactivates
and normally contains the entire sequence of emotional
states which assure the individual of his own, his parents', the entire world of objects' 'goodness' and the
hope of fulfillment of love in the face of frustration, hostility, and normal ambivalence."[34]

Kernberg describes further "the couple's intuitive
capacity to weave changing personal needs and experiences into the complex net of heterosexual and homosexual, loving and aggressive, aspects of the total relationship expressed in unconscious and conscious fantasies
and their enactment in sexual relations."[35] Like Balint,
he writes movingly of the transcendent potential of love,
of "the 'coming alive' of inanimate objects—the back-

ground figures of human experience—illuminated by a love relation. This reaction to inanimate objects, as well as to nature and art, is intimately connected with the transcending aspect of a full love relation. . . . the capacity to experience in depth the nonhuman environment, to appreciate nature and art, and to experience one's self within a historical and cultural continuum are intimately linked with the capacity for being in love . . . falling in love represents a developmental crisis powerfully favoring the deepening of these other potentials."[36]

Kernberg is careful to insist that heterosexuality itself does not necessarily accompany or result from psychological health. In fact, he argues, sexual inhibition is often a progressive *result* of reaching the triangular oedipal level of development, when genital prohibitions become meaningful. By contrast, those with borderline pathology may achieve genital enjoyment as a flight from orality, precisely because their pathology goes along with splitting and idealization: "The capacity for sexual intercourse and orgasm does not guarantee sexual maturity, or even necessarily represent a relatively higher level of psychosexual development. . . . Clinically one finds that the full capacity for orgasm in sexual intercourse is present both in severe narcissistic personalities and in mature people and that sexual inhibition is present both in the most severe type of narcissistic isolation and in relatively mild neuroses and character pathology."[37]

Yet even though his characterization of mature love does not specify object choice, Kernberg assumes that mature love will be heterosexual. He does not say why such gender complementarity is necessary; he only asserts that it is. He refers to "the capacity for tenderness and a stable, deep object relation with a person of the other sex"; to a total object relation "including a complementary sexual identification"; and to the fact that mature love requires "resolution of oedipal conflicts"—

explicitly in the first two cases, implicitly in the third, privileging heterosexual object choice.[38]

I have suggested that within psychoanalysis there are no grounds for considering homosexuality but not heterosexuality as a symptom. But we also know that like Freud—who describes sexual variation in case studies and descriptive accounts as well as (for example, in his three "Contributions to the Psychology of Love") defensive qualities in prevalent heterosexual patterns—psychoanalysts normalize heterosexuality. They do this by tying the developmental story of heterosexuality to the psychology and culture of normative gender, and thus they are able to differentiate abnormal from normal in contrasting homosexuality and heterosexuality.

There are two paradigmatic accounts here. The first tendency within this literature ties sexual object choice to gender identification, but it does not really explain erotization. It more or less empties heterosexuality of intense erotism, thereby contrasting it with homosexuality and the perversions, where intense erotism is central. A second tendency explains heterosexual erotism by embedding it in male dominance—and in so doing implicates in normal heterosexuality not just gender but gender inequality as well. Heterosexuality either definitionally requires and means acceptance of such inequality, or it developmentally seems to entail such dominance and submission.

Both sorts of accounts formulate things differently for the cases of homosexuality and heterosexuality. For homosexuality (or perversion) they tell a story about what went wrong to produce the deviation, for heterosexuality, a less explicit account of what needs to go right. We are back in the domain of Freud's original theories: gender identity and sexual orientation are conflated, and biology has self-evident psychological meaning. Also as in Freud's original account, this privileging of heterosexuality by normalizing gender exhibits little intrinsic relation to other aspects of any theorist's characterization of sexual object choice.

According to Kernberg, identification with the same-sex parent is an oedipal task: "Women . . . are to cross the final boundary of an identification with the oedipal mother. . . . Men have to cross the final boundary of the identification with the oedipal father."[39] He is explicit about the relation between this "achievement" and normative social conformity, tying a "full sexual identity" or "normal sexual identity" (meaning gender identity and heterosexual object choice) to "reciprocal sexual roles and . . . full awareness of social and cultural values." He argues that a "stable sexual identity and a realistic awareness of the love object" include "social and cultural in addition to personal and sexual ideals."[40] Gender identity and cultural role identification thus build into and are requisite for heterosexual development.

Like Kernberg, Person has developed her account of romantic love in the first instance without explicit gender-normative claims. Love is characterized by a "leap out of objectivity and into subjectivity." It involves "sharing in each other's subjective realities." Love "denies the barriers separating us, offering hope for a concordance of two souls . . . 'emotional telepathy.' . . . [It is] an emotion of extraordinary intensity. . . . The experience of love can make time stop. . . . [It] may confer a sense of inner rightness, peace, and richness; or it may be a mode of transforming the self. . . . [It is] a mode of transcendence . . . a religion of two."[41]

Person notes that the longing for love usually crosses perceived difference—"otherwise the lover has essentially chosen a narcissistic love object and the enormous transcendent power of love is lost"—but she points out that humans can vary in ways other than in their biological sex: for example, in age, background, culture, interests, abilities, character.[42] At the same time, she assumes heterosexual love and follows the dominant psychoanalytic model in accounting for its development.[43] Each person experiences "a developmental series of 'love dialogues'" beginning with idealization of the mother, following through a family romance to idealization and identification with outsiders. In the "normal" course of development, the child consolidates her or his identification with the same-gender parent, and this identification enables and fuels desire for the opposite sex. Gender identification here leads to opposite-sex object choice as a "complementary" relationship replaces an identificatory relationship. Adolescents, in transition, may desire the heterosexual love object of their best friend, because their identification rather than a sense of complementarity shapes desire, but "in the normal course of development . . . the yearning that attaches to idealization is transformed from the wish *to be like* (or to replace) to the wish *to be with*. . . . desire shifts toward complementariness."[44]

There are two major problems with accounts that tie the development of heterosexuality to identification. First, they provide no sense of the *motivation* for such shifts in identificatory choices. We are left to assume something natural, not in need of motivational explanation, in identification with the same-gender parent. More important, such accounts do not explain how *identification*—an ego choice that might well tell the developing child whom he or she *ought* to love in order to be like the identificatory object—relates to erotization. If appropriate sexual object choice comes from identification with the same-gender parent, it is almost an aspect of role-modeling. But erotization here seems to run counter to object choice: attachment to the identificatory object, a homoerotic object, is foremost in the psyche such that, in the boy's case, love for the father

and attachment to *him* leads the boy to take the mother
or women as object. The shift toward complementariness is described as a prevalent developmental pattern
but is not explained.[45]

French psychoanalytic theory provides a second perspective on the tie between gender and heterosexual development. This theory ties heterosexuality more to
passion, conflict, and erotism than do Kernberg's and
Person's identification theories, but it relates heterosexuality not only to gender difference but also to sexual
inequality and power; gender inequality and power difference in fact become the sine qua non of heterosexual desire. Chasseguet-Smirgel, for example, claims an
identity between "the universe of differences" and "the
genital universe" and considers that the pervert refuses
the "(genital) universe of difference." Echoing Jacques
Lacan, for whom genital difference is implicitly un-
equal, constituted as law exclusively by the father, she
claims that the genital universe is also the "paternal
universe [of] constraints of the law" and that the pervert wants to "dethrone God the Father."[46]

McDougall asserts that normal heterosexuality requires acknowledgment of the bipolarity of the sexes, of
the primal scene, of castration, and of genital difference
as the basis of sexual arousal: "The belief that the difference between the sexes plays no role in the arousal of
sexual desire underlies every neosexual scenario." Like
other writers, she recognizes the universal prevalence of
bisexuality and a desire to possess the genital organs of
both sexes, but such bisexuality must rest on recognition of a sexual difference privileging heterosexual phal-
locentrism: "The phallus, symbol of power, fertility, and
life, must . . . come to represent, for both sexes, the image of narcissistic completion and sexual desire. . . .
should a symbolic phallic image be entirely missing, psychotic confusion about sexual relationships would en-
sue." Thus, "neosexual inventions . . . attempt to short-

circuit the multiple effects of castration anxiety." In implicit linguistic support for her asymmetrical view, McDougall refers to the relation of the (named) "father's penis" and the (unnamed) "mother's sexual organ" (the translation is her own).[47] Thus, as for Lacan, "inscription" in the gender system is the same thing as inscription in a (hetero)sexual subjectivity that privileges the phallus.[48]

Kernberg, who warns analysts against identifying "with a traditional cultural outlook" toward sexual roles and inequality, nonetheless follows French theory. According to him, a boy's oedipal complex can be impeded by a mother who has rebelled against the "'dominance' of the paternal penis and the 'paternal law' in general," and a girl's progress toward heterosexuality can develop only with difficulty, as her mother withholds vaginal sexuality from her and keeps it for herself. "The mother's implicit denial that her daughter has genitals" leaves the girl alone and in private with her sexuality, turning to her father in "intuitive longing" for penetration by a penis that would confirm her own vaginal genitality and female sexuality. Such processes are interfered with further if the mother herself has conflicts about the female genitals and genital functions.[49]

Non-French theorists agree with French theory that heterosexuality encodes male dominance, but they are likely to see this as a probable or prevalent developmental compromise rather than as a developmental task. Person, a leading feminist analyst who is critical of male dominance, nonetheless implies in *Dreams of Love* an acceptance of an almost necessary inequality in heterosexual relations. She suggests that a power differential in love may be ineradicable: insofar as women long for love and men fear it, normal heterosexuality will tend to include female submission and male domination or, more tentatively, women will distort love in the direction of the former and men in the direction of the

latter. Such a tendency originates in cultural impera-
tives, early object relations, and the asymmetric structures of the Oedipus complex; it finds reflection in
transference patterns, in which women erotize relationships with men in authority and seek the shelter of power, and men split sex and dependency and need the safe-
ty of a power advantage. As a developmental outcome,
"women are more at ease with the mutuality implicit in
love, as well as the surrender, while men tend to interpret mutuality as dependency and defend against it by
separating sex from love, or alternatively, by attempt-
ing to dominate the beloved."[50] Person here points to
congruence with our society's dominant romantic fantasies, suggesting that culture embeds itself in even as it
also grows out of defensive structures and intrapsychic
patterns.[51] She also implies that these modes of relationship are themselves defensive structures, based on
felt need and attempts at resolution of anxieties, fears,
and conflicts.

A feminist critique, of course, would challenge any
normative practice that requires or seems to elicit male
dominance, and normative heterosexuality has been
widely criticized on this ground as has a psychoanalytic
theory that seems to require it.[52] But we can also find
grounds internal to psychoanalysis for problematizing
the psychoanalytic account: the *asymmetry* in heterosexual desire, and its intertwining with patterns of
dominance and submission, begin to indicate its defensive features and symptomatic nature. Susan Contratto
and Jessica Benjamin provide the developmental and
clinical story of this defensive compromise, in which
women's heterosexuality is formed through overvaluation and idealization of the father accompanied by submission and compromise. They locate the origin of girls'
difficulties in infancy, when mother and father are both
present and psychologically important, though in dif-

ferent ways, and Contratto's account also documents how such patterns continue throughout childhood.[53]

Benjamin focuses on the period in the separation-individuation process, the rapprochement subphase, when girls and boys are struggling with autonomy from their mother. Because rapprochement coincides with an early genital phase, classic rapprochement preoccupations with agency and independence become tied to sexuality and gender. Separation-individuation theorist Margaret S. Mahler has noted that girls tend to respond during this phase with depressive affect and a sense of helplessness.[54] Benjamin argues that this is not a direct response to the discovery of genital difference; rather, their common gender with their mother does not allow girls to use their father as boys do, to represent and mediate independence and separateness. For both boy and girl, during the rapprochement phase and later, the father represents active desire and the mother a more desexualized regression. As the boy resolves the rapprochement crisis, his father acts as a vehicle for separation and as a model of activity and desire: "In rapprochement," says Benjamin, "the little boy's 'love affair with the world' turns into a homoerotic love affair with the father, who *represents* the world."[55] By contrast, the girl (as McDougall also suggests) must represent her own sense of desire by something that is not hers and not feminine. Her desire—even when allowed to develop by a father who enables identificatory love—is alienated, because male sexuality and the male genitals, with their symbolic intertwining of agency and separation, represent excitement and erotism.

Contratto draws upon her clinical work to illuminate father-daughter relationships in which the daughter is allowed to develop just such an idealizing love. She describes the working fathers of a number of her women patients, to all intents and purposes "good" fathers ("model fathers of the '40s, '50s, and '60s")—who ener-

getically returned to the household evenings and week-
ends bringing treats; who engaged in exciting adven-
tures and interactions; who needed to be carefully ca-
tered to when short-tempered or preoccupied; and who
contrasted with taken-for-granted, everyday mothers.
These fathers' "presence was an event in their daughters' lives." They made "their daughters feel special,
cosy, and cared for [and were] exciting and fun, . . . especially . . . in comparison to their mothers." These
daughters learned from their own experience, maternal
teaching, and observation of their mothers not to cross
such fathers—to squelch disappointment or censure, to
accept criticism and belittlement, not to intrude on paternal space. Contratto's clinical account accords with
the traditional theory, in which female sexuality is not
active or autonomous but passive in relation to the father and men in general. Several patients, she claims,
"spent a great deal of energy trying to figure out what
sort of woman the man she is interested in *really* wants
so that she can be that kind of woman." They also denied felt difference: "speaking up in a relationship, even
if only to acknowledge a difference, carries with it great
fears." One patient assumed that "independent pleasure
and excitement was disloyal."[56]

Complementing this distortion of authenticity in female desire is a problematic masculinity. Benjamin and
Contratto emphasize how fathers collude in their presen-
tations of self as special, exiciting, and powerful, and other researchers note that fathers prefer boy babies and develop a more intense bond with them.[57] Extending some
of my own writing about defensive masculinity, Benjamin shows us how males develop a "false differentiation"
from their mother, resting on denial of the mother's subjectivity and objectification of her. Objectification and
the difficulties faced by the boy who wants recognition
and response from his mother, on whom he at the same
time does not want to be dependent, twist into a need to

dominate women, into the erotization of domination in the normal case and into erotic violence in the abnormal. The psychoanalytic sociologist Miriam Johnson contrasts the girl's gendered oedipal change of object—from mother to father—with what is symbolically a generational change on the part of the boy—from passive, less powerful son in relation to mother, to active, more powerful man in relation to less powerful women.[58]

Benjamin and Contratto posit that these solutions on the part of both women and men undermine female sexuality. Women find it difficult to integrate agency and love and often accept whatever love they can get in exchange for identification with and love from a man. The unavailability of the father as a reliable presence (less available to his daugher than to his son, less available to her than a mother to her son) leads girls, in the normal case, to develop tendencies toward an idealizing love for their fathers that forms the basis of their heterosexuality. Such love pulls toward submission, overvaluation, masochism, and the borrowing of subjectivity from the lover.[59]

Identification with the same-sex parent, then, differs for the girl and the boy. A boy can come to his own heterosexual position through an idealizing love for an exciting father who makes himself available (a paradox pointing us to a link between homoerotic identificatory love and heterosexual object choice). The boy's oedipal and preoedipal relations with his mother ensure that such sexuality will require objectification and power—that is, will undermine true object love. The girl's situation is different. "Power," notes Contratto, "has a gender: charismatic power with its excitement, visibility, and privilege is male. Maternal power, characterized by reliability, nurturance, and the capacity for comfort, is female."[60] Benjamin adds that the mother tends not to be seen psychologically or portrayed culturally as a sexual subject; she is there to serve the child's interests, and her sexual power is frightening and denied.[61] Thus, for the girl, identification is likely to be—at best—with her mother's maternality rather than with her mother as an active sexual being. Moreover, the mother may have made a similar bargain in her own development and may therefore also experience her own sexuality as passive and submissive. If the daughter identifies with her mother's sexuality in this situation, she identifies with compromise and submission.

In looking at psychoanalytic accounts of gender and heterosexuality, one has the sense that with the exception of Contratto and Benjamin, they are undermined by the taken-for-grantedness of both biosocial gender and cultural male dominance. How does identification with one parent lead to erotic desire for the other? How do we reconcile a complex and varied view of the multiplicity of sexualities and the problematic nature of conceptions of normality and abnormality with a dichotomous, unreflected-upon, traditional view of gender and gender role or an appeal to an undefined "masculinity" and "femininity"? Assumptions about cultural normality, conformity, and biological function and cause are allowed to stand in a way that would rarely happen with regard to other features of psychic functioning or development.[62] A psychic wish, "need," or tendency to be dominant or submissive is not problematized; inherent inequality and hierarchy of role and valuation between two kinds of people and their genital constitution are taken for granted; and those who do not accept such inequality and hierarchy are seen as neurotic or perverse, engaged in special pleading or a refusal to accept nature. One's own psychology is taken as model of normality and desirability.

Even the language used to describe homosexual development often presumes heterosexual structures of attraction. Developing homosexual boys are "feminized," as if it is only by being feminine that someone could desire a male; developing lesbians are "tomboys," since one has to be masculine to desire women. While the evidence of fantasy and behavior disentangles gender and sexuality, psychoanalytic theory often assumes their unity.[63]

I have suggested that we know, or conceptualize theoretically, much more about the homosexualities and perversions than we do about what we take for granted to be most people's sexuality, and that what we do know about this normal sexuality indicates that it is difficult to privilege it in evaluative psychological terms. On the "healthy" or "mature" end of the spectrum we can conceptualize forms of homosexuality in which the quality of object relationship (in terms of wholeness, respect for the other, and so forth) is equivalent to that of our conceptions of mature heterosexuality. Equally, we can conceptualize homosexuals who can fully differentiate their gender identity (unless this identity requires heterosexual object choice) and who have a firm and relatively unproblematic sense of gendered self (I use "relatively" here only to stress that *no one's* sense of gendered self is entirely unproblematic). On the more symptomatic end of this same spectrum, we have accounts that demonstrate the inherent conflict, domination, trauma, and "perversion" in normal heterosexuality. These perspectives converge to suggest that normal heterosexuality has the same kind of dynamic and developmental ingredients as *all* sexuality.

This theoretical conclusion accords with clinical experience, which demonstrates—whatever our cultural and biological assumptions may be—that the sexual stories, conscious and unconscious fantasies, and transference processes of heterosexuals are as complex and individualized as those of homosexuals. If we do not hold such a position, we give up a lot theoretically and methodologically, and we compromise our clinical stance and capacity. Erotic feelings, conflicts, defenses, accounts of relationships with parents, attempts to sort out a self, accounting for what gives pleasure and why or for what is desired and what fantasied—and the developmental and transferential history of all these—are the bread and butter of clinical work. We find clinical stories both wild and tame, people who are focused on or obsessed with sexuality and those who are not (the latter likely to be "normal" heterosexuals who can take their sexuality culturally for granted), but we always find a story. *Clinically, there is no normal heterosexuality.* Any heterosexuality is a developmental outcome reflected in transference, whatever admixture of biology or culture may contribute to it and however we define "culture" (as gender identity, sexual rules, dominant cultural fantasies, or mother's and father's conscious and unconscious gender identifications). This developmental and transferential outcome results from fantasy, conflict, defenses, projections and introjections, regressions, the making and breaking of relationships internally and externally, and attempts to constitute a stable self and maintain self-esteem. Whatever our theoretical approach—classical, structural, object-relational, Kleinian, or self-psychological—sexual development and orientation, fantasy and erotism, need explaining and describing in the individual clinical case.

We return to the two opening elements in my argument. First, I have been able to elicit in the literature some accounts of normal heterosexuality, but compared with the luxuriant richness of clinical accounts and general theories about deviant sexualities of many sorts, we must be struck by the relative paucity of case studies and clinical observations of "normal" heterosexuality, as well as by the underdevelopment of general theory about it. Second, in the sphere of transference and developmental understandings that emerge from the clinical situation, we cannot find a reason to differentiate heterosexuality or to see homosexuality as more of a defense or compromise formation. Logically and methodologically, we find that when we do have a clinical or developmental account of heterosexuality, either it is relatively empty and uninteresting, or it makes heterosexuality—as an object of inquiry and understanding, and as an experience—into whatever we want to say any sexuality is.

A final objection to the argument in this chapter could still be raised: is there not a difference between a normal, everyday defense or compromise formation and a disorder or symptom, since we know that all psychic products and processes involve defense and compromise formation? There probably is, and many clinicians can probably differentiate what we might want to call "perversion" of the homosexual and heterosexual (as well as bisexual, celibate, or autoerotic) variety from what we might want to call "normal," object-related homosexuality and heterosexuality. At least, following Stoller, we can delineate the extremes.

But following certain authors' lines of delineation demonstrates the limitations and difficulties of such a strategy. Many accounts of perversion stress the driven intensity, the insistent and narrowly specific object choice and sexual aim, and the necessity to repeat. McDougall, for example, singles out the compulsive and addictive qualities of the neosexualities as they fulfill the multiple needs of a "complex psychic state in which anxiety, depression, inhibitions, and narcissistic perturbation all play a role."[64] What follows from this view is that normal heterosexuality is less intense, more diffuse, and affectively flatter. Many heterosexuals would not agree, nor does what we learn from clinical experience, literature, or our own and our acquaintances' lives. What would we make, in this view, of such compelled lovers from literature as Tristan and Isolde, Antony and Cleopatra, Anna and Vronsky, Heathcliff and Cathy, Othello, Gabriel García Marquez's Florentino Ariza?[65] As clinicians, we can easily demonstrate their "neurosis"—compulsive drivenness, narrowly specific object choice, perversity (the main point of García Marquez's book is that love is a disease—in his case, a cholera)—but this leaves us explaining the passion, intensity, addiction, and obsession of all lovers' desire in terms of perversion.

After we factor out the "perverse" elements in these examples of obsessive, intense, erotic heterosexual passion, whatever remains seems (to be blunt) boring. We are left to infer either that the subjectively important and intense parts of all sexual experience and fantasy are perverse or symptomatic, or that addiction and compulsion may be ingredient to all intense sexual experience and fantasy. If we take the first point of view—arguing that only the noncompulsive, nonaddictive parts of sex constitute normal heterosexuality and that the rest is "perversion"—we still need individual, detailed, complex accounts to explain the mix that is both intense and flat. The traditional psychoanalytic account that distinguishes "perverse" from "normal" sexuality does not do that. We will still be hard pressed to distinguish between passionate, homoerotic, true object love (with whatever "true object love" should include, as indicated by Balint, Kernberg, Person, and others) and passionate, heteroerotic, true object love. Alternatively, many accounts imply that distinctions about compulsion, addiction, narrowness of aim and object, intensity, and so forth, do better in differentiating male sexuality in general (whether homosexual or heterosexual) from female sexuality in general. In this case, it is women, both heterosexual and lesbian, who find themselves on the noncompulsive, nondriven, nonintense (verging on sexless) end of the spectrum of sexual desire.

Similar considerations hold true, I believe, for the issue of humiliation. Stoller puts humiliation at the core of perversion and also at the core of sexual excitement in general. We might, as Stoller suggests, turn to the outcome of the sexual excitement—does it lead to sustained intimacy or not?—but this will not distinguish all homosexualities from heterosexuality, and it certainly differentiates among heterosexualities as well. (We might also wonder—at the risk of idealizing and de-sexualizing women—about the extent to which hostility and the desire to harm are more characteristic of the sexual fantasies and practices of men than of women, since "perversion" as well as actual and fantasied sexual violence, abuse, and rape seem more widespread among men than among women.)[66]

A variety of other pathological, symptomatic elements—weak self-other differentiation, narcissistic object choice, severe reaction to narcissistic injury, conflictual or not firmly established gender identity, problematic body image, and borderline or narcissistic or even psychotic ideation and character—are thought to distinguish homosexuality and perversion from heterosexuality.[67] The focus on the early origins of deviant sexualities has enabled a pathologization of these sexualities, since in psychoanalytic developmental theory we have tended to correlate the degree of pathology with the earliness of a trait's origins.[68] Such a focus may also have been fostered by theorizing on the basis of a clinical population as well as by lack of scrutiny of the origins of apparently normal—because behaviorally typical—heterosexualities.

In any case, the problem here is that heterosexual object choice and heterosexual behavior can characterize the most disturbed individual (indeed, as noted above, Kernberg, has more hope regarding love relations for what we think of as the more disturbed borderline personality than for the narcissist).[69] Furthermore, we have only to recall Freud's "Case of Homosexuality in a Woman" to remind ourselves that many homosexualities are of oedipal (therefore later developmental) origin. There is no inherent incompatibility between postoedipal "true object love"—concern for the wishes of the other, capacity for whole object relations, and an established gender identity (unless we *define* this gender identity as including heterosexual object choice)—and homosexual object choice, even if there are many homosexuals, as there are heterosexuals, who do not have these capacities.

Whether we take Freud's bifurcate model of the complete Oedipus complex or Lewes's twelvefold model, we have only a variety of ad hoc criteria for privileging one postoedipal outcome over the other, or over eleven others, all of which involve assumed ties among biological sex, gender, and sexuality. The assumptions underlying these criteria, reviewed throughout this chapter, are, first, a presumed biological normality; second, identification with the right parent in the right way—in which case erotic desire and passion emerge somehow out of identification, or sexual orientation is no more than gender role acceptance; third, acceptance of cultural values; fourth, a theoretical assumption that satisfactory gender differentiation *means* sexual orientation; fifth, acceptance of an a priori given valuation of the phallus as a sign of sexual difference and gender hierarchy, entailing the beliefs that there is one right outcome to castration anxiety and that sexual desire must incorporate and reproduce sexual inequality. (If one argues in this last case that the acceptance of hierarchy and inequality is ego-syntonic—consonant with the ego-ideal—one then confronts the argument for ego-syntonicity in various alternative sexualities.) There are, as I indicate, problems with all these assumptions.

It seems, finally (and analytic writers occasionally imply as much), that there is a spectrum of qualities of object-relatedness, erotization, compulsiveness, drivenness, castration anxiety and other anxieties about bodily and genital intactness, imaging of gender, specificity versus broadness of object choice and sexual aim, denial or defense, character pathology or neurosis, conjoinings of fantasy and reparative goals in both those who make heterosexual and those who make homosexual object choices. Any evaluation according to such criteria as compulsiveness, addictiveness, humiliation, or the presence or absence of a "true object relationship" will apply to some people expressing each of these sexual orientations.

The second part of my argument simply noted the paucity of clinical accounts that problematize or focus on heterosexuality and of theory about heterosexuality. Psychoanalysts cannot claim that homosexuality is more symptomatic than heterosexuality without better accounts of the latter (and the accounts we do have suggest that we will not find that it is).

But I am of course also suggesting that psychoanalysts would do well to investigate heterosexuality for its own sake. As I begin to indicate in the next chapter, there are very good reasons (having nothing to do with what is normal and what is not) for building our complex clinical understandings of individual cases into a more complex theory, for challenging our simple normative model of one modal boy and one modal girl who develop into "normal" heterosexuals, for assuming that we will find instead a wide variety of "normal" heterosexualities, just as we know there are many homosexualities and many heterosexual perversions.

In provocative or ironic response to occasional analytic reference to homosexuality as a symptom, my previous working title for this chapter was "Heterosexuality as a Symptom." But my beliefs are in fact less absolute. I believe we must reserve judgment about the "symptomatic" nature of heterosexuality or of some heterosexuals and the "normality" of some homosexualities or homosexuals; in this chapter, I have argued that such differentiation, given our current clinical and developmental knowledge, is not possible. I also reserve judgment on final causes in any individual case. The ways in which sexual orientation, organization, fantasy, and practices result from biology, from cultural valuation and construction, from intrapsychic solutions to conflict, from family experience, and from gender identity may well vary from one person to another.

Some psychoanalytic or gay theorists or activists might want to argue either that heterosexuality is morally superior or politically better for society (that some people must behave heterosexually some of the time for species reproduction is self-evident but does not explain the individual and cultural variety and specificity I alluded to earlier), or that for moral or political reasons we must defend any sexuality.[70] But I think we must be quite clear about the nature of this kind of argument: psychoanalytic theory does not give us a basis for answering such moral and political questions.

It is not impossible that we may at some time find grounds, from a psychoanalytic point of view, for evaluating the relative "healthiness" (for example, symptom freedom, lack of pathology, or secondary autonomy) of homosexuality and heterosexuality; though such a position is certainly controversial and not accepted by many sexual activists, I do not myself argue for a total psychological relativism. As McDougall, Stoller, and others make clear, there are probably good grounds within psychoanalytic clinical theory for making comparative evaluations among sexualities. But at this stage in our knowledge, these grounds do not differentiate homosexuality and heterosexuality, and my own expectation is that they will not do so in future. Currently, when we make evaluative claims, we do so in the context of a normative cultural system that includes a set of biological assumptions, probably one in which normal sexuality means not only essentializing and absolutizing gender and sexual difference but also sustaining gender inequality. If we retain passion and intensity for heterosexuality, we are in the arena of symptom, neurosis, and disorder; if we deperversionize heterosexuality, giving up its claim to intensity and passion, we make it less interesting to theorists, clinicians, and practitioners. This chapter suggests that we treat all sexuality as problematic and to be accounted for.

3 Individuality and Difference in How Women and Men Love

The preceding two chapters have laid out tensions and conflicts in psychoanalytic theories and ideologies of sex and gender. In "Heterosexuality as a Compromise Formation" I pointed out that psychoanalysis provides us a normative—and an empirical (that is, one based on clinical observation)—story that ties heterosexuality to male dominance and sexuality to gender. I also suggested that as psychoanalysts move from contrasting men and women to contrasting heterosexual and homosexual, they tend both to bracket and to assume gender difference. In contrasting normal heterosexuality with homosexuality, gender is minimized and prevalent gender differences in sexuality and love disregarded, so that "heterosexuals" can be contrasted with "homosexuals," whether male or female. At the same time, a modal (and model) femininity and masculinity are also assumed. This modal (and model) engendering pervades psychoanalytic writing since Freud. Yet, as "Freud on Women" documented, there is in Freud's writings a dual (or multiple) vision: on the one hand, "normal" femininity; on the other, many women, many possible female developmental outcomes, many prevalent attitudes, fantasies, and fears on the part of men toward women.

This chapter moves among these various claims, though it does not resolve them. In the background there are generalizations: psychoanalysts, like people in everyday life, seem to observe prevalent differences between men and women. They also observe and theorize, even if they do not critique, the connections between gender, erotism, prevalent and normative heterosexuality, and male dominance. But psychoanalytic theory, like much academic psychology and virtually all the popular psychology literature, has tended to overgeneralize and universalize—to oppose all men to all women and to assume that masculinity and femininity (and their expressive forms) are single rather than multiple. This is a peculiar tendency in a field whose data are by necessity so resolutely and intractably idiographic, so individual and case-based.

Sexual love is a particularly useful arena for investigating the multiple intersections of gender and sexuality and for seeing the connections of culture, ideology, and psyche. In what follows I claim—against generalization—that men and women love in as many ways as there are men and women. Without losing sight either of the privileging of heterosexuality in culture and psychoanalysis or of the psychological and cultural pervasiveness of male dominance, I suggest why it is difficult and problematic to generalize about how women and men love.

For clinicians, sexual love presents a special challenge. It is a fulcrum of gender identity, of sexual fantasy and desire, of cultural story, of unconscious and conscious feelings and fears about intimacy, dependency, nurturance, destructiveness, power, and powerlessness, body-construction, and even of self-construction. It may be—along with and connected to anyone's sense of self as child (those unconscious and fantasy sequelae of individual psychobiography), men's sense of self as masculine, and women's sense of self as mother—one of the most complexly constructed of the many deeply felt, deeply conflicted issues that our patients present us and, more generally, that people in our society experience. A blending of culture and psyche, of cultural meaning and

personal meaning, makes love complex in particular
ways. These complexities entail that our typical clinical
focus on intrapsychic elements (as if these can be contrasted with or considered apart from the external
world and culture) misses a large part of what goes to
constitute love. As I begin to suggest in Chapter 2, any
particular man or woman chooses particular objects of
desire or types of objects, and has particular types of
love experiences, and in each case we need to give a cultural *and* an individual developmental story of these
patterns and choices. More specifically, to account fully
for these choices we need to give a story of how, among
its other processes and patterns, individual development—drawing from constitutional endowment, early
and later intrapsychic experience, and internal and external processes of object relationship—chooses from,
reacts to, ignores, interprets, and modifies culture.

This chapter suggests some very general axes of variation, or ingredients, which it behooves clinicians and theorists to consider as we try to unravel how particular
women and men (our patients, ourselves, our friends,
those we interview, those we read about in fiction or
nonfiction)—and women and men more generally—love.
We are more likely to notice tendencies toward which we
have been sensitized. As my earlier discussions imply, I
believe that we have not been sensitized to psychological
variation and complexity, which have by and large been
missing ingredients in psychoanalytic accounts and psychoanalytically based feminist accounts of normative or
typical gender and sexuality (both psychoanalytic and
gay and lesbian accounts of gay and lesbian sexuality, by
contrast, have been more respectful and attentive to variation).[1] Yet even here, as I move to suggest alternative formulations and to stress individuality and difference, I
also stress that we in turn run the risk of noticing only
these newly discovered tendencies and selecting those
elements that fit this previously thought-of template,

thereby keeping us as practitioners from fully understanding our patients and as theorists from enriching
and changing our theories.[2]

One element in love, the particular sense of self and
relationship that comes from the individual family in
which someone grows up and that gives any individual's love uniqueness, is familiar to us from clinical work
and psychoanalytic theory. Clinicians are used to focusing on this factor, both as we reconstruct it historically
and as we experience and analyze it in the transference.
Through such analysis we excavate all aspects of a particular person's psychological makeup: her or his prevalent defenses, unconscious fantasies, projective and in-
trojective constructions of self and objects, and so forth.
We know that any particular patient comes from a particular family with a specific cultural background, but
those of us who are Euro-American and middle class
tend to take this background for granted if we share it
with our patients. We seek to figure out how a particular mother or father was experienced, and we assume
cultural setting, rather than working to elucidate, for
example, how a particular parental relationship was
typical of a particular subculture or cultural enclave.
What matters becomes not so much the cultural practice, conception, or self-conception as how the child experienced it.

Such a culturally blind strategy is in all likelihood
generally problematic, but in the case of love, as in the
case of gender, stopping with individual particularity
especially occludes understanding.[3] Love has an added
cultural resonance, especially through its links with
gender and with cultural beliefs about sexuality, that
makes stopping with personal or familial meaning sin-
gularly inadequate. As I noted earlier, in our society today no one can grow up without, from earliest childhood, shaping a sense of love from fairytales, myths,
tales of love, loss, and betrayal, movies, books, and tele-

vision. These cultural stories and fantasies are experienced directly, and they are personally recreated through fantasy and the emotional and cognitive reshaping of introjections. They are also mediated by conscious and unconscious parental fantasies and patterns of projection and by emotional communication between child and parents. As parents read or tell stories or share movies, they themselves consciously or unconsciously experience such cultural fantasies in relation to sexual partners, to themselves, and to their children.

Stories of passion, sexual desire, and fulfillment are found in all cultures, but heterosexual erotic love as we read, see, and hear about it in contemporary Euro-American culture is a specific cultural product. Many cultures do not have such a concept, and even in Western civilization erotic love floats around historically: it is marital and heterosexual in some eras, extramarital in others, heterosexual and tied to notions of intimacy in the current period, passionate (though questionably genital) between women in the nineteenth century, erotic between older men and younger boys in classical Greece, normatively carnal today, and normatively reserved for spiritual love of Christ in the Middle Ages. Even "Judeo-Christian" culture splits, as Judaism finds marital sexual passion desirable and prescribed (under conditions of extensive ritual control), whereas the classic Christian position holds all sexual excitement and lust to be undesirable, if unavoidable.[4]

Cultural resonance and cultural saturation ensure that sexual and romantic fantasies, mediated as they partially are through language, will incorporate cultural stories. These cultural stories and their psychological specifications often entail commonalities that allow us to label some man's or woman's fantasy by gender, but these fantasies are so culturally loaded that we run grave risks in saying that *this* is how men and women love—as if such fantasy is a product of biological or psychobiological endowment. In a different culture, or within different subcultures in our own, how men and women love varies tremendously.

In some cases, we can define through exclusion. The clinically observed gothic heroine, or "Rebecca," fantasy—self-devaluing or masochistically tinged love involvements or obsessions with unavailable, angry, domineering, or distant partners, including the fantasy of transforming these partners into gentle lovers—seems a feminine form of love. When we find such a fantasy in a man (which we most certainly will), whether in relation to women or to other men, we may claim that this man loves in a feminine manner. But to regard the Rebecca fantasy as feminine does not imply that all women experience love in this way, just as it does not imply that men never do. A "Portnoy" fantasy—obsession with a devouring, hysterical mother which pushes a man toward reserved, distant women with characteristics distinctly unlike those of that mother, or toward men—seems a generally masculine fantasy but certainly does not characterize how all men love. These two examples both specify how some women and men love and indicate how the form of such love fantasies—partaking as they certainly do of individual familial and psychological history— takes added shape by the availability of *Rebecca* (itself perhaps an adolescent "Beauty and the Beast" story) and *Portnoy's Complaint* (itself built on centuries of Jewish mother stories, as well as on fairytales and other stories of terrifying and sexually or maternally engulfing women).[5] We are here in the realm of "subjective" and "objective" gender: these fantasies may involve unconscious or conscious subjective identifications as feminine or masculine, and they may also more typically characterize how men love or how women love.[6]

We also get at the importance of the cultural input to love by comparing cultures. Here I draw implicitly upon my clinical experience and explicitly upon women's writings to examine mainly women's culturally shaped experiences, but I believe my point about individual and cultural variation and specificity holds for men as well. Contratto and Benjamin (see Chapter 2) articulate a prevalent theme in Euro-American psychoanalytic feminist writing on love. From clinical experience and observation they describe the way mothers subtly and indirectly build up and idealize fathers to their daughters, perhaps by complement effacing themselves. In Lacanian and non-Lacanian French psychoanalytic writing, what American feminists criticize as indirect subtlety becomes the explicit injunction that mothers stress paternal and phallic primacy. I quoted Chasseguet-Smirgel and McDougall above: children must come to recognize a genital universe which is also the "paternal universe [of] constraints of the law"; sexual difference and normal heterosexuality are by necessity tied to "the phallus, symbol of power, fertility, and life, [representing] for both sexes the image of narcissistic completion and sexual desire."[7] Of course, we also find a protest and the rejection of such a position in the writings of Hélène Cixous and Luce Irigaray, but their very protest attests to the cultural and psychological power of such developmental injunctions and fantasies.[8]

In the United States, Latina writing on sexuality portrays, though critically, a similar situation to that invoked by French theorists, implying that male dominance is more culturally valorized and elaborated in Latino than in Anglo culture. Oliva Espín and Cherríe Moraga describe mothers who directly teach their daughters that women are inferior and men superior, that daughters should submit to and serve their father and brothers, and that the penis is the valued genital and sexual organ.[9] My own clinical experience and cross-cultural reading suggest that variations of this directly taught sexual inequality and subservience to men may be pervasive in those cultures that the Turkish sociologist Denise Kandiyoti calls "classic patriarchy"—in China, India, North Africa, the Muslim Middle East, and perhaps much of the circum-Mediterranean.[10] At the same time Latina writings, rather than articulating a Euro-American bewilderment about how to find "women's desire" within a seeming sexlessness (itself perhaps a heritage from nineteenth-century Protestant notions of women's passionlessness), describe a Mexican cultural legacy portraying women as temptresses whose evil sexuality betrayed Aztec men to the Spanish conquerors—that is, as Aztec Eves.[11]

By contrast, African American mothers do not seem to teach their daughters subservience to men. In at least one survey, African American daughters report that their mothers warned them to be wary of men and marriage and stressed men's unreliability and undependability.[12] Such warnings about men of the same racial-ethnicity who are sexual tempters and betrayers come in the context of even stronger warnings and terror about potential abuse by white men.[13] At the same time, in some traditions—that of the blues, for instance—we find assertion of a strong black female sexuality and sexual desire.[14]

I do not mean these very brief examples to serve as generalizations about women's and men's love in these different cultures. I cannot claim the cross-cultural knowledge even to begin to do so; indeed, the intention of this chapter is to indicate that such culturally specific generalization would be highly problematic. Such examples can suggest, however, that if even a few women from these different groups have different unconscious and conscious senses of female self, body, and sexual fantasy and different cultural stories of male-female relations, and if a few men from these different groups have related stories, then already we have variation in how women

and men love. Some middle-class Euro-American wom-
en's sexuality differs from that of some French women,
who love differently from some Latinas, who experience
men differently from some African American women.

My point is that we are partially on the ground of
culture, story, and language when we talk about how
men and women love. In turn, these stories and this language always include conceptions of gender and sexuality. For this reason, to query how women and men
love yields more than a descriptive account of tendencies and patterns—that men love in particular ways,
women in others. As Freud's original account of femininity suggests, we must also characterize *gendered subjectivity* (which often includes senses of sexuality) in relation to love. Women and men love as psychologically
and culturally gendered selves, with gender identities
and sexual desires (and inhibitions and prohibitions)
that they consciously and unconsciously experience and
enact.

Our understanding of these processes has been ham-
pered by clinicians' tendencies to separate inner and
outer too absolutely. Some clinicians and psychoanalytic theorists would argue that by looking at culture and
language I am moving away from the psychoanalytic
realm, with its unique focus on unconscious mental processes. But such a perspective is misguided. It does not
take account of how unconscious fantasies and senses of
self and identity are formed: what cultural and interpersonal experiences interact with or are available for
those innate psychological capacities and potentialities
that enable us to form a self with emotional capacities
and conflicts, to develop a particular gender identity
rife with individual and cultural psychological meaning,
and to organize drive potentialities into individual erotic
desire. Others believe that we can predict how women
and men love from anatomical givens and their automat-
ic psychological sequelae. Some, finally, rest their case

on a psychoanalytic theory (for example, most Lacanian-inspired readings of psychoanalysis) that reifies "the unconscious" as a sui generis, autochthonous entity that is apart from culture and the symbolic. (As I point out later, those culturalists who claim that culture predicts forms of sexuality, gender, and love also have only a partial perspective.)

I argue here, by contrast, that an important ingredient in any woman's or man's love or sexual fantasies, erotic desires, and behavior will be found in her or his particular unconscious and conscious appropriation of a richly varied and often contradictory cultural repertoire, which has been presented directly through what we think of as cultural media and indirectly (again consciously and unconsciously) through parents, siblings, and other early parental figures. We recall the Wolf Man and the Rat Man, both of whom formed their love and sexuality in important ways in relation to servant women, thereby infusing with images of class superiority and inferiority the contempt for women that Freud takes to be characteristic of the normal oedipal resolution. There are many cultural masculinities and femininities and masculine and feminine love stories, and people form their fantasies and desire for individual reasons from one or another or from none of these.

Of course, one consistent thread runs in varied ways throughout many of these psychological and cultural stories: most men and women must come to psychological terms with male dominance. Men have social and familial power and cultural superiority; in the psychoanalytic view—one mirrored in most of my examples—they have sexual dominance as well. Somewhere along the line, often but not always in relation to the father, part of learning the meanings of masculinity and femininity includes learning not just difference but differential value and asymmetrical power and hierarchy. Family dynamics, as these reflect cultural and personal meaning and as identity and desire are constituted, link sexuality (particularly heterosexuality) to a psychology and culture of gender such that inequality and power difference become part of the cultural and psychological requisites that must be negotiated in (though they do not directly construct) sexual desire and love. As I noted earlier, one cannot find general psychoanalytic accounts of the development of heterosexuality that do not include gender inequality and male dominance.

But such inequality is not monolithic. Robert Connell suggests that we distinguish analytically between "hegemonic" and "subordinate" (alternative) masculinities and femininities. Hegemonic masculinity organizes itself around psychological, cultural, and social dominance over women (Freud's normal male oedipal outcome), but it also organizes between masculinities, enabling dominant males to dominate subordinate males culturally, psychologically, and even sexually. Tomás Almaguer reminds us that in Latin American culture the *activo* homosexual position is not stigmatized, whereas the *pasivo* position is.[15]

Hegemonic psychological masculinity takes many expressive forms: there is the heterosexual who refuses permanent sexual commitment, moving from partner to partner in a more or less exploitive way; there is the "good" husband and father who works at a steady job to support a family. Alternative masculinities might include the new gentle feminist man and a variety of homosexualities. There is no hegemonic cultural femininity that defines itself as dominant over men, but alternative femininities can emphasize either subordination and compliance or sexual assertiveness and independence. Femininities can also make men more or less central; my brief account of Latina and African American women's writing portrays such a contrast, and it seems possible that some middle-class women of today's generations are more centered—in some cases, perhaps, defensively—on

work identities than were women of older generations.[16]
Or, different femininities may substitute an emphasis on
maternal love as a center of identity for an emphasis on
heterosexual femininity. Sometimes there is also, as my
example of black maternal teaching makes clear, a wom-
en's culture (currently mirrored in some feminist writing
and found in much nineteenth-century feminism as well)
which, in the context of male social domination, claims
personal and moral superiority over men. Parents may
communicate any of these patterns covertly or overtly as
a child forms her or his gendered sense of self and desire.

We now add that women and men from all groups
may love people of the same gender rather than of the
other gender. If we see these love relationships in gendered terms, then one partner must love according to
the one gender and the other, presumably, according to
the other: the "butch" and "femme" member of the lesbian pair, or the "active" and "passive" partner in the
gay couple. Still other accounts conflate same-gender
erotic choice with gender identity, claiming that lesbians love like a man—in a masculine fashion—and
stressing the "effeminacy" of boys who become gay. But
if we acknowledge that some women love like men and
some men like women, we are claiming that there are at
least two polar opposite modes in which people of *each*
gender can love. We hold on to a putative descriptive
generalization (or prescriptive claim) concerning modes
of male and female love (active versus passive, dominant versus submissive) at the expense of being able to
describe how these particular, actual, men and women
love. If we claim that lesbian relationships replicate
mother-daughter patterns, whereas heterosexual wom-
en love as they loved their fathers, we now have three
different relational stances in female love: mother of the
daughter, daughter of the mother, and daughter of the
father. Lewes, as we have seen, points to *twelve* possible
oedipal constellations and outcomes for the boy; half of

these are heterosexual, but only one is what we normatively think of as how men love.

We can now turn more directly back to the psychodynamics of the family, but without forgetting what we
have just established: that these psychodynamics include, unconsciously and consciously and among other
elements, cultural patterns and meanings. How women
and men love will be heavily influenced, though not determined, by their navigation through the relationships
and fantasies of early childhood, and this is the terrain
that we think of as more typically psychoanalytic.

Much of my previous writing provides an account of
how girls and boys differentially negotiate these early
experiences, particularly in terms of their relationship
to their mothers. I have argued that girls, like boys,
form their first love relationship, fantasies, sense of self
and gender, and modes of love and desire through that
relationship. I suggested that most girls seek to create
in love relationships an internal emotional dialogue
with the mother: to recreate directly the early infantile
or oedipal connection; to reconcile, rescue, or repair; to
attack, incorporate, or reject; to emancipate themselves
or define themselves against her.[17] I have yet to come
across any woman patient, or any narrative (fictional,
autobiographical, biographical, or poetic) written from
the daughter's point of view—among patients or writers of whatever sexual orientation and from whatever
cultural group—for whom in the broadest sense we
could say that "love" for a daughter's mother was not
central.[18]

Women seek directly to reconstitute, resurrect, reshape, reimagine an emotional relation with their mothers; they fantasize and unconsciously experience internal
and actual mothers even as they form relationships with
men. Part of "how women love" concerns the (never absolute but always shifting) resolution of this desire (as well
as of envy, anger, hatred, ambivalence, or whatever other

strong emotions toward and internal representations of her mother a woman may have) and its "level" of resolution (adolescent, preadolescent, latency, oedipal, preoedipal, or some combination) for the individual woman.[19] I do not think that this aspect of female love is necessarily subjectively gendered. A woman's feelings, fantasies, and self-construction in relation to her mother—coming as they do from perverbal and preoedipal preoccupations with self-other differentiation, the relation to the breast, the managing of anxiety, and so forth, as well as from preoedipal and oedipal subjectively gender-linked experiences—may or may not have to do with a sense of self as female or conscious or unconscious fantasies about gendered sexual desire. But that a woman is preoccupied intrapsychically with her mother as an internal image and object, and that this intrapsychic preoccupation helps shape her love relationships (and much else about her intrapsychic and interpersonal life), are near-universal clinical observations.

Those aspects of men's love that grow out of their relationship to their mothers are more likely than women's to be subjectively gendered: that is, to be intertwined for a man with his sense of (cultural and personal) masculinity. Although the early relation to the mother may not be gendered from the boy's subjective viewpoint (whereas his mother's subjective relation to him is certainly so)—coming as it does from a period before a boy can *have* a subjective sense of gender—this relation is inevitably transformed by his learning (in his own idiosyncratic way, personally charged by his own individual emotional constructions) of cultural and personal gender. Freud argues that this personal appropriation of cultural gender is a central outcome of the oedipal resolution for boys, as boys learn that the meaning of masculinity and the penis is their superiority to femininity and the lack of penis. But recent theorists and researchers have suggested that this learning of the value of gender difference is an earlier developmental process, more closely tied to development in the second year.[20] By contrast to Freud's, Klein's accounts of the defensive constructions of gender and of fantasies of male superiority in boys and girls in what she calls the "early stages of the oedipus conflict" tends to accord with this contemporary developmental account.[21]

The subjective gendering of masculine love in relation to the mother is not neutral. Subjective gendering for men means that such love defines itself negatively in relation to the mother as well as in terms of positive love and attachment; as I suggested earlier, insistent masculine superiority and asymmetry in (hetero)sexuality indicate a defensive construction. We do not need to go far in the psychoanalytic literature (we begin with Horney's classic statement) or in the popular media to read about men's fear of women, female sexuality, and the intimacy and nurturance that evoke the early dependent relation to the mother—a fear particularly noteworthy in a situation of such clearly claimed and institutionally supported cultural and psychological superiority. Though we may find comparable female fear of male sexuality or power—of being penetrated, violated, attacked, or overwhelmed, for example—this fear is in accord with rather than in opposition to dominant cultural and social constructions of gender.[22]

Thus, if a first ingredient in how women and men love comes from a personal appropriation and transformation of cultural stories and fantasies, a second seems to arise from their negotiation of their relationship to their mother, or to a female caretaker and primary love object. I cannot address the infinite recursiveness here: of course, the mother herself is also culturally and personally gendered, but this is not the whole aspect of her being and fantasy or the whole of what goes into the individual mother-child relationship. This relationship to the mother tends to become more pervasively tied to meanings of gender for men than for women, though it certainly becomes tied to such meanings for women as well. Moreover—at least in the Freudian cases, as well as in literary and theoretical writings on interracial and interclass nursing and nannies—the intrapsychic putting together of the relationship to early female caretakers can also be tied to class and racial splits in erotic love, thereby shaping active desire, avoidance, perversion, and one version of the erotic and symbolic splitting between good and bad women and erotic and idealized love that Freud first described.[23] Some writing by Euro-American lesbians (for example, Rich's *Of Woman Born*) suggests the direct connection of desire to experience with women from caretaking and servant classes (the connection that we find in some men).[24] But although many women for various reasons repeatedly choose male love objects from different racial-ethnic or class groups, I have not seen clinical or literary descriptions of racial or class splitting entering into women's heterosexual desire as a direct result of actual early experiences with men of different classes or races. This may be an artifact of my limited reading, but it may also be a result of men's tendency not to be primary caretakers or an effect of cultural taboo.

Generally, the relation to the mother comes to symbolize for both sexes either nurturance or its rejection, intimacy or its transformation, body pleasure or body shame, guilt at independence or resentment at dependence. Passivity or activity, aggression and submission, may also enter in. I stress that these are *aspects* of the relationship that *tend* to be psychologically symbolized and accorded emotional meaning in later love, but that there is *no single way* in which they are worked out for women in contrast to how they are worked out for men. Each woman and man negotiates *some* of these aspects of her or his particular relation to her or his particular mother or early female love objects and caretakers.

It is thus a mistake to claim that *the* mother symbolizes or emotionally organizes something particular or generates particular kinds of fantasies, or that she must act in a particular way: that, for example, this unitary entity symbolizes castration; or that she represents "the" preoedipal oneness, "the" holding environment, or an inevitable total dependence; or that *her* "lack" is necessarily contrasted with the father's phallus or her baby-gestating capacities with *his* lack. There is no such uniformity in early childhood experience; recursively, any individual mother's appropriation, creation, and integration of her femaleness, maternality, and selfhood will have, in her development and current psychological life, the same contingent construction as that of her children. As cultural summaries, moreover, these descriptions generalize and universalize without warrant and exclude emotional meaningfulness.

To return to Freud and all analysts who reflect on Oedipus is to ask about the father, a third relational and fantasy ingredient in how women and men love. The father certainly falls under the cultural symbolizations of gender that I discussed earlier, and a large body of research suggests that he himself tends to participate actively in this cultural symbolization and placement. If we wish to understand how a man or a woman loves, insofar as gender is relevant to this loving we would make a great mistake not to look at that person's relation to his or her father (if one is in the psychological or actual picture, and whether or not he is in the household). As it turns out, fathers are themselves intensely interested in gender and gender difference, so that if one parent can be said to "create" gender in their children or to help in that creation, it is the father. The research literature suggests that fathers (to put it simply) prefer boys, interact more with them, and emphasize gender-differentiated behavior in sons and daughters more than do mothers. If marital tension increases, differentiated behavior increases: fathers become more authoritarian toward and rejecting of daughters as they gain less satisfaction from their wives. They are also more likely to stay in marriages that have produced sons.[25]

As Chapter 2 suggested, insofar as the father-daughter relationship contributes to how women love, many girls walk a kind of tightrope. A father may wish his daughters to be more "feminine" (traditional psychoanalytic accounts suggest a seduction that is not a seduction to help create heterosexuality in girls), but at the same time he is likely not to be as interested in them as he is in his sons, or as a mother is in daughters and sons. This leads to a feminine idealization of men and constraint on assertion of desire. The girl learns to put up with less from him and from men than she really wants, takes what she can get rather than what she wants in the way of attention and affection. Yet in the absence of primary male figures, girls seem to find it hard to develop a confident sense of self in relation to men—and we seem to prefer, whatever a girl's sexual preference, that she make sexual-love choices as much as possible proactively rather than defensively and reactively.[26]

A primary way in which the closely intertwined cultures of gender and love may enter the family and the child's unconscious, then, is through the father. Part of any investigation of how women and men love must include, in any particular case, attention to how this gender, power, and paternal appreciation or lack of appreciation for a child were experienced and helped shape a self.

These tendencies in daughters' reactions to paternal personality and behavior that the research and theoretical literature report, however, are not universal. In my clinical experience, some women are quite comfortable excoriating a father's aggression, sexism, self-absorption, and overcontrol, whereas it is a painful guilt more than they can bear to acknowledge any sense of a mother's failure or limitation. Other women and girls, by

contrast, find it easy to criticize and reject mothers—
who they are certain have the strength to survive their
onslaught—whereas they protect perceived paternal in-
adequacy and weakness. Women's and men's fantasies
and feelings about fathers also seem to be shaped, consciously and unconsciously, by cultural factors, so that
women from classic patriarchal cultures, for example,
tend to have a stronger sense of paternal domination
and preference for sons or a stronger conscious ideology
of paternal perfection.

I do not here assert, as I and others have previously
claimed, that women fall in love rationally, putting up
with flaws in male lovers as they learned to accept
whatever love or attention they could get from fathers. I
suggest, rather, that these widely observed paternally
generated dynamics and fantasies should be floating
through clinicians' (interviewers', readers', self-analy-
sers', theorists') minds as potentiality when we hear our
patients express love—as, for example, our women patients may image furious, rejecting divorced fathers,
whirlwinds of power and anger, fathers who devalued
their daughters' efforts to become strong and powerful,
or fathers who expressed preference for them as latency-
aged bright feminine androgynes. (For years, most studies of "successful" women indicated this sort of suppor-
tive, encouraging, seductive father behind the success:
Louisa May Alcott succeeded in spite of, and Alice James
may have failed because of, a domineering father.[27])

Nor do I suggest that men automatically or universally
bask in the glory of father preference, always express gender superiority in love through paternal identification,
or enter the adult world of love with an unproblematic
sense of male superiority and masculine sexual aggression. Masculinity, intimacy, conflicts about sexual poten-
cy, anger, resentment—all these may confound how a
man loves, and mediation by the father is *one* aspect to be

investigated. For example, did a man's father seem forever passive and unavailable as a model? Was he available at all or withdrawn into work, another marriage, depression, or an active single life? Was he intensely desired for his power? Did he conform to cultural stereotypes of successful masculinity? Did he submit himself to the mother and/or protect his son from her?

In an earlier writing, "Oedipal Asymmetries and Heterosexual Knots," I described how the particular developmental pathways and resulting constellations of capacities and needs for intimacy differ in men and women and lead to prevalent tensions and strains in heterosexual relationships. Many readers of that article and my own clinical experience affirm that the tensions and strains I described reflect many men's and women's experience.[28] This "asymmetry" in heterosexual experience has also been described by feminist theorists, often drawing on psychoanalysis, in terms of the inequality between men and women in society, culture, and the family.

Recently, though, feminist theory has also taught us to be wary of generalizations about gender difference, and it is this wariness that I urge in this book. I do not claim that generalization is never useful clinically; I have written about gender differences, and I take the usefulness of these insights for granted. Feminist philosopher Marilyn Frye suggests the helpful concept of pattern here and urges us toward epistemological "strategies of discovering patterns and articulating them effectively, judging the strength and scope of patterns, properly locating the particulars of experience with reference to patterns, understanding the variance of experience from what we take to be a pattern." Patterns help give meaning to and interpretively situate particularity ("make our different experiences intelligible in different ways").[29] By contrast, generalizations can easily be misread as universal claims, as applying to all men versus all women and as describing an essence of gender that does not respect the very great individual and cultural differences among women and among men.

I wish to advocate caution about how to *use* generalizations and to specify what a generalization can claim. As I note in the beginning of this book, there has been within psychoanalysis, as in our everyday social, and cultural world, a tendency to turn generalizations into universal claims and polarizations—to speak of male versus female, "the boy" or "the man" versus "the girl" or "the woman"—and, indeed, to search for gender differences while ignoring commonalities and similarities. Such generalizations can draw our attention away from the very great similarities between some men and some women and among people in general, and from the arenas of psychological, social and cultural life in which gender or sexuality are not prominent.[30] Clinically, expectations and theories of gender difference often cloud, delimit, and threaten to occlude our vision.

Alternatively, we wipe out difference (and inequality): sex is sex, love is love, and we talk in general ways about how humans experience desire or sexual love. My claim is that gender makes a difference but does so in particular ways. Gender identity and fantasy, however we want to define them—whether we are men or women, how we conceptualize ourselves, our desires and our possibilities—make an enormous difference, for our patients (if we are clinicians) and for ourselves. But though each person's gender is centrally important to him or her, consciously and unconsciously, it does not follow that we can contrast all women, or most women, with all or most men. Moreover, the ways people conceptualize themselves as gendered vary with a number of factors, including culture, history, and early family development—the specifics of *their* family and its meanings as they fantasize and create this family, as they experience engulfment, separateness, destruction, threat, love, hate. What becomes important to an individual is not just femaleness or maleness but the psychologically and culturally *specific* meanings that gender holds *for that individual.*

The problem, then, is how to consider gendered subjectivity without turning such a consideration into objective claims about gender difference. To look at *constructions of gendered experience* within the perceived relations of gender is not the same as looking at difference and similarity; subjective (conscious and unconscious) *meanings* of love and attachment are not the same as objective behavioral or clinical observations turned into generalizations and then universal claims—against which we then judge normality and abnormality, into which we then fit our particular patients or the subjects of our research or theory.

This chapter has begun to untangle the complex interactions of gender-inflected factors in sexual love and the patterns of gendered identity and meaning that can help us to interpret these specificities: male dominance as a pervasive cultural, psychological, and social phenomenon; myriad cultural fantasies and stories; gender identity and identifications as subjective features of psychological life. Gender is an important ingredient in how men and women love, and all men's and women's love fantasies, desires, or practices are partially shaped by their sense of gendered self. But this sense of gendered self is itself individually created and particular, a unique fusion of cultural meaning with a personal emotional meaning that is tied to the individual psychobiographical history of any individual.

We must investigate individually how any person's sexual orientation and organization, erotic fantasy, and practices result from anatomy, from cultural valuation and construction, from intrapsychic solutions to conflict, from family experience, and from gender identity. All these will enter the individual case of how any woman or man loves. To factor out the variations I have described in order to get at what remains and "really" differentiates how women and men love misses the point. It misses the point in the clinical situation, where we are called upon to respect individual complexity, and it misses the point in theory as well. A variety of patterns of attachment and fear, erotic and romantic fantasy, imaging of one's own and the other's sexual anatomy and gender, specificity versus broadness of love choice and sexual aim, aggressive or reparative and intimacy-seeking goals are found in any man or woman—all these patterns exhibiting varying degrees of defense or conflict-freedom and accompanying all levels of character pathology and neurosis. These patterns and processes both draw from and reshape cultural stories, and how this is done also varies in the individual case. To understand how men and women love requires that we understand how any particular woman or man loves; to understand femininity and masculinity and the various forms of sexuality requires that we understand how any particular woman or man creates her or his own cultural and personal gender and sexuality.

Freud, despite his theoretical predilections, also used his clinical experience to portray gendered and sexual variability and to challenge cultural and psychoanalytic normalizing. Careful clinicians and theorists have followed his lead in this respect. Psychoanalysts have nearly unique access to many people's sexual fantasies, identities, and practices. We should use this access to help us fully understand gender and sexuality in all their forms.

Notes

1. Rethinking Freud on Women

1. For an overview of modern psychoanalytic writings on women, see Nancy Chodorow, "Psychoanalytic Feminism and the Psychoanalytic Psychology of Women," in *Feminism and Psychoanalytic Theory* (Cambridge: Polity Press, and New Haven: Yale Univ. Press, 1989), 178-98. For some history of early critiques, see Susan Quinn, *A Mind of Her Own: A Life of Karen Horney* (New York: Summit Books, 1987).

2. Daniel N. Stern, *The Interpersonal World of the Infant* (New York: Basic Books, 1985), 19. Stern distinguishes the "clinical infant" and the "observed infant." I borrow his distinction here.

3. Sigmund Freud, "The Dissolution of the Oedipus Complex," in *Standard Edition of the Complete Psychological Works of Sigmund Freud* (hereafter *S.E.*), ed. James Strachey (London: Hogarth Press, 1953-74), 19:173-79; "Some Psychical Consequences of the Anatomical Distinction between the Sexes," *S.E.* 19:248-58; "Female Sexuality," *S.E.* 21:225-43; and "Femininity," *New Introductory Lectures on Psycho-Analysis*, chap. 33, *S.E.* 22:112-35.

4. Ruth Mack Brunswick, "The Preoedipal Phase of the Libido Development," in Robert Fleiss, ed., *The Psychoanalytic Reader* (New York: International Univ. Press, 1948), 231-53.

5. Freud, "Femininity," 135.

6. Ibid., 126.

7. Freud, "Dissolution of the Oedipus Complex," 178.

8. Freud, "Some Psychical Consequences," 252-53, 255.

9. Freud, "Analysis Terminable and Interminable," *S.E.* 23:250-53.

10. See Jeanne Lampl-de Groot, "The Evolution of the

Oedipus Complex in Women," in *The Development of the Mind: Psychoanalytic Papers on Clinical and Theoretical Problems* (New York: International Univ. Press, 1965), 3-18; and Helene Deutsch, *The Psychology of Women*, vol.1, *Girlhood* (New York: Grune and Stratton, 1944), which summarizes Deutsch's earlier work.

11. Freud, "Female Sexuality," 226, 229.

12. See Helene P. Foley, ed., *The Homeric Hymn to Demeter: Translation, Commentary, and Interpretive Essays* (Princeton: Princeton Univ. Press, 1993).

13. Freud, "Female Sexuality", 229. According to Elizabeth Young-Bruehl (*Anna Freud* [New York: Summit Books, 1988], chap. 2), there is good reason to believe that Freud's clinical model here—the girl who compulsively masturbates as she struggles with penis envy and, presumably, penis preoccupation, as well as the girl who leads him to "credit a single instance" ("Some Psychical Consequences," 256) of the masculinity complex—is Anna Freud, whose first analysis preceded Freud's writing of "'A Child Is Being Beaten': A Contribution to the Study of the Origin of Sexual Perversions" (*S.E.* 17:175-204), and whose second analysis just preceded his writing of "Some Psychical Consequences." I discuss the complexities of the clinical bases of Freud's theories of femininity below.

14. Freud, *Fragment of an Analysis of a Case of Hysteria* ["Dora"], *S.E.* 7:3-122. On Dora, see Charles Bernheimer and Clair Kahane, eds., *In Dora's Case: Freud—Hysteria—Feminism* (New York: Columbia Univ. Press, 1985); and Hannah S. Decker, *Freud, Dora, and Vienna 1900* (New York: Free Press, 1990). On Dora as an adolescent, see Erik H. Erikson, "Reality and Actuality: An Address," in *In Dora's Case*, 44-55. On Dora's name, see Jane Gallop, "Keys to Dora," in *In Dora's Case*, 200-220, and Hannah S. Decker, "The Choice of a Name—'Dora' and Freud's Relationship with Breuer," *Journal of the American Psychoanalaytic Association* 30 (1982): 113-36.

15. Josef Breuer and Sigmund Freud, *Studies on Hysteria*, *S.E.* 2:21-47.

16. Freud, "The Psychogenesis of a Case of Homosexuality in a Woman," *S.E.* 18:145-72, and *Introductory Lectures*, *S.E.*, vols. 15 and 16.

17. Breuer and Freud, *Studies on Hysteria*, 103.

18. Ibid., 176.

19. Freud, "Case of Homosexuality," 147, and *Introductory Lectures*, 16:261-64, 264-69.

20. See Nancy Chodorow, "Seventies Questions for Thirties Women," in *Feminism and Psychoanalytic Theory*, 199-218; and Chodorow, "Where Have All the Eminent Women Psychoanalysts Gone? Like the Bubbles in Champagne, They Rose to the Top and Disappeared," in Judith R. Blau and Norman Goodman, eds., *Social Roles and Social Institutions: Essays in Honor of Rose Laub Coser* (Boulder: Westview Press, 1991), 167-94.

21. Karin Martin develops the concept of "sexual subjectivity" in "Feminism, Sexual Subjectivity, and a History of Women's Orgasm in the West," a gender/feminist tutorial paper prepared for Sociology Preliminary Examinations, 1991, and "Puberty, Sexuality, and the Self: Gender Differences in Adolescence," her Ph.D. dissertation in progress.

22. Many feminists have pointed to the lack of maternal subjectivity in Freud in particular and psychoanalytic theory in general. Among classical writers, Melanie Klein and Alice Balint perhaps come nearest to describing the psychology of mothering, and many clinical accounts—though not Freud's—also describe, if they do not theorize, maternal feelings. Klein, in "Mourning and Its Relation to Manic-Depressive States (in *Love, Guilt and Reparation and Other Works* [New York: Delta, 1975], 344-69)," describes in great detail a mother's reaction to her son's death. Phyllis Grosskurth, in *Melanie Klein: Her World and Her Work* (New York: Knopf, 1986), 251, claims that this mother is Klein herself. And see Alice Balint, "Love for the Mother and Mother Love," reprinted in Michael Balint, *Primary Love and Psycho-Analytic Technique* (New York: Liveright, 1965), 91-108.

23. Daphne de Marneffe, "Looking and Listening: The Construction of Clinical Knowledge in Charcot and Freud," *Signs* 17 (1991): 71-111, suggests that Freud's clinical technique was an important part of this process: he listened to hysterical patients (with however prejudiced or theory-shaped an ear) rather than simply looking at them and classifying them, as had Jean Charcot. One listens to subjects; one looks at objects.

24. Freud, "'Civilized' Sexual Morality and Modern Nervous Illness," *S.E.* 9:177-204.

25. Freud, *Introductory Lectures*, 16:352-54.

26. Freud, "Three Essays on the Theory of Sexuality," *S.E.* 7:125-243, and "Case of Homosexuality," 151, 158, 147, 150.

27. Freud, "Case of Homosexuality," 170, 169.

28. Breuer and Freud, *Studies on Hysteria*, 178-81.

29. Freud, "The Dynamics of Transference," *S.E.* 12:97-108.

30. Breuer and Freud, *Studies on Hysteria*, 160.

31. See Karen Horney, "The Flight from Womanhood: The Masculinity Complex in Women as Viewed by Men and by Women," and "The Dread of Women," both in *Feminine Psychology* (New York: Norton, 1967), 54-70, 133-46; and Melanie Klein, "Early Stages of the Oedipus Conflict," in *Love, Guilt and Reparation*, 186-98, as well as her post-Freudian writings such as "The Oedipus Conflict in the Light of Early Anxieties," in *Love, Guilt and Reparation*, 370-419, and "Envy and Gratitude," in *Envy and Gratitude* (New York: Delta, 1975), 176-235.

32. Freud, "Fetishism," *S.E.* 21:153. I have rearranged the structure of Freud's sentence to make it active and to fit into my own sentence, but I have not changed his words. The original phrase is, "the portion of his narcissism which Nature has, as a precaution, attached to that particular organ."

33. Freud, "A Special Type of Choice of Object Made by Men" and "On the Universal Tendency to Debasement in the Sphere of Love" are his first two "Contributions to the Psychology of Love" (*S.E.* 11:163-90).

34. Freud, "Femininity," 133-34.

35. Freud, "Fetishism," 152.

36. Freud, "Medusa's Head," *S.E.* 18:273-74.

37. Freud, "Fetishism," 154.

38. Kenneth Lewes, in *The Psychoanalytic Theory of Male Homosexuality* (New York: Simon and Schuster, 1988), 78, points out that all preoedipal children are psychically male homosexual, since they are imaged by Freud to be sexually phallic and sexually desirous of a phallic mother.

39. Freud, *The Interpretation of Dreams*, *S.E.* 4:96-121.

40. On Grusha, see Freud, *From the History of an Infantile Neurosis* ["The Wolf Man"], *S.E.* 17: 90-96. On Fräuleins Peter and Lina, see *Notes upon a Case of Obsessional Neurosis* ["The Rat Man"], *S.E.* 10:160-61.

41. "The Rat Man," 197-98.

42. Freud, *Civilization and Its Discontents*, *S.E.* 21:72, 68.

On oneness in the early infantile relationship to the mother, see Freud, "On Narcissism: An Introduction," *S.E.* 14:67-102.

43. Freud, *Introductory Lectures*, 16:314.

44. Freud, "Femininity, 133.

45. See Carl J. Jung and Karoly Kerenyi, *Essays on a Science of Mythology: The Myth of the Divine Child and the Mysteries of Eleusis* (Princeton: Princeton Univ. Press, 1963); and Erich Neumann, *The Great Mother*, 2d ed. (Princeton: Princeton Univ. Press, 1963). On Hera in the masculine psyche, see Philip Slater, *The Glory of Hera: Greek Mythology and the Greek Family* (Boston: Beacon Press, 1968).

46. Freud, "The Taboo of Virginity (Contributions to the Psychology of Love, III)," *S.E.* 11:191-208.

47. Ibid., 198-99.

48. Freud, "Some Psychical Consequences," 257.

49. Shoshana Felman, "Rereading Femininity," *Yale French Studies* 62 (1981): 21. Felman also points out that accounts by women, like my account here, are really asking, "What does the question 'What is femininity—*for men?*' mean *for women?*"

50. Horney, "Flight from Womanhood," esp. 57-60 and 70.

51. Marie Bonaparte, *Female Sexuality* (New York: International Univ. Press, 1953).

52. See n. 13 above. On the autobiographical bases of Deutsch's and Anna Freud's writings, see Helene Deutsch, *Confrontations with Myself* (New York: Norton, 1973); Paul Roazen, *Helene Deutsch* (New York: Anchor, 1985); Nellie Thompson, "Helene Deutsch: A Life in Theory," *Psychoanalytic Quarterly* 56 (1987): 317-53; and Young-Bruehl, *Anna Freud*. On Bonaparte, see Celia Bertin, *Marie Bonaparte* (New York: Harcourt Brace Jovanovich, 1982).

53. See Quinn, *A Mind of Her Own*; and Grosskurth, *Melanie Klein*.

54. Freud, "Femininity," 135, and "Female Sexuality," 226.

2. Heterosexuality as a Compromise Formation

1. This chapter is not a review of the literature but, as a quick check on these impressions about psychoanalytic attention to sexuality, Karin Martin surveyed eight major psychoanalytic journals for the past ten years, finding only a couple of articles on love, and a few that address heterosexuality tan-

gentially. (David W. Hershey, "On a Type of Heterosexuality, and the Fluidity of Object Relations," *Journal of the American Psychoanalytic Association* 37 (1989): 147-71, stands out as one article that takes heterosexuality as problematic.) Martin's conclusion (personal communication): "It struck me that it is not just normal heterosexuality that is neglected by psychoanalysis but more specifically normal male heterosexuality. Female sexuality, heterosexual or not, has been continuously understood as problematic if not deviant by psychoanalysis, and there are accounts of how and why it is so problematic."

2. A large contemporary historical and theoretical literature documents persuasively the relatively recent construction of such notions of sexual identity or of sexuality. Formerly, Western culture conceptualized sexuality in terms of individual prescribed and proscribed acts, and the terms and conceptions of "homosexual" and "heterosexual" as unitary stances, kinds of persons, or object choices were unknown. See Michel Foucault, *The History of Sexuality*, vol. 1, *An Introduction* (New York: Pantheon, 1978); Jonathan N. Katz, *The Gay/Lesbian Almanac* (New York: Harper and Row, 1983); Katz, "The Invention of Heterosexuality," *Socialist Review* 20 (1990): 7-34; Arlene Stein, "Three Models of Sexuality: Drives, Identities and Practices," *Sociological Theory* 7 (1989): 1-13; and Jeffrey Weeks, *Sexuality* (London: Tavistock, 1986).

3. See, e.g., Ethel S. Person, *Dreams of Love and Fateful Encounters: The Power of Romantic Passion* (New York: Norton, 1988); Otto Kernberg, "Barriers to Falling and Remaining in Love," in *Object Relations Theory and Clinical Psycho-Analysis* (New York: Aronson, 1976), 185-213; Kernberg, "Mature Love: Prerequisites and Characteristics," in *Object Relations Theory*, 215-39; and Kernberg, "Boundaries and Structures in Love Relations," in *Internal World and External Reality* (New York: Aronson, 1980), 277-305. For an earlier period, see Michael Balint, "Eros and Aphrodite," 59-73, "On Genital Love," 109-20, and "Perversions and Genitality," 136-47, all in his *Primary Love and Psycho-Analytic Technique* (New York: Liveright, 1965). Balint and Kernberg address sexuality and, in Kernberg's case, aggression, specifically. See Balint, "Eros and Aphrodite" and "Perversions and Genitality"; Kernberg, "Between Conventionality and Aggression: the Boundaries of Passion,"

in Willard Gaylin and Ethel Person, eds., *Passionate Attachments: Thinking about Love* (New York: Free Press, 1988), 63-83; Kernberg, "Aggression and Love in the Relationship of the Couple," *Journal of the American Psychoanalytic Association* 39 (1991): 45-70; and Kernberg, "Sadomasochism, Sexual Excitement, and Perversion," *Journal of the American Psychoanalytic Association* 39 (1991): 333-62,

4. Katz, in "Invention of Heterosexuality," 10, 14, provides useful historical insight into this problem, pointing out that the first medical writer to use the term "homosexual" referred exclusively to gender conceptions ("persons whose 'general mental state is that of the opposite sex'"). He also suggests that the turn-of-the-century term "invert" allows gender-crossing—deviation from True Womanhood and True Manhood—to stand for homoerotic desire. Karin Martin, in "Gender and Sexuality: Medical Opinion on Homosexuality, 1900-1950," *Gender and Society* 7 (1993): 246-60, reviews the medical and psychiatric literature and finds that gender behavior, physiology, and sexual orientation are intertwined in discussions of homosexuals of both sexes. Theoretically, as I noted in the preceding chapter, Freud construed gender identity and personality almost exclusively as issues of sexuality.

5. Kenneth Lewes, in *Psychoanalytic Theory of Male Homosexuality*, 232, suggests that modern psychoanalysis, uncharacteristically, does just this, defining homosexuality in terms of its behavior rather than its dynamics or phenomenology.

6. E.g., noted psychoanalytic feminist Juliet Mitchell, in "Eternal Divide," [London] *Times Higher Education Supplement*, Nov. 17, 1989, 20, takes me to task for claiming that the "distinction between the sexes . . . is neither necessary nor universal," and she goes on to assert: "The problem of the social and psychological reproduction of heterosexuality for the propagation of the species comes after that. . . . for reasons of heterosexuality, all societies have made some, however different, distinction between the sexes which has, so far, been universal and necessary."

7. Stoller, *Observing the Erotic Imagination* (New Haven: Yale Univ. Press, 1985), 101.

8. Ernst Kris, "The Personal Myth," *Journal of the American Psychoanalytic Association* 4 (1956): 653-81.

9. On the effects of culturally hegemonic beauty concepts, see Robin Lakoff and Raquel Scherr, "Beauty and Ethnicity," in their *Face Value* (Boston: Routledge, 1984), 245-76.

10. I cannot consider here the whole question of hormonal and genetic impact on gender-typed behavior. My point is simply that people labeled as girls tend to desire males, and people labeled as boys, to desire females, in both cases regardless of chromosomal or hormonal makeup. See the classic studies of John Money and Anke Ehrhardt, reported in *Man and Woman, Boy and Girl* (Baltimore: Johns Hopkins Univ. Press, 1972). My general argument is that dynamic, individual issues will be important, whatever our final conclusions about biologic input to sexual orientation.

For a more extended discussion and review of the literature about the connections between prenatal and postnatal hormones, brain development, genes, and sexual orientation, see William Byne and Bruce Parsons, who in "Human Sexual Orientation: The Biologic Theories Reappraised," *Archives of General Psychiatry* 50 (1993): 228, claim that "there is no evidence at present to substantiate a biologic theory, just as there is no compelling evidence to support any singular psychosocial explanation." They advocate a complex "interactional model in which genes or hormones do not specify sexual orientation per se, but instead bias particular personality traits and thereby influence the manner in which an individual and his or her environment interact as sexual orientation and other personality characteristics unfold developmentally" (236-37) and stress that "conspicuously absent from most theorizing on the origins of sexual orientation is an active role of the individual in constructing his or her identity" (236). See also Suzanne Kessler's remarkable study, "The Medical Construction of Gender: Case Management of Intersexed Infants," *Signs* 16 (1990), 3-26, which finds that doctors in such cases assign sex not primarily on the basis of chromosomes or hormones, but on the possibility of constructing a penis or vagina that can engage in heterosexual intercourse.

Some commentators believe that the evidence supports biological influence in particular cases; e.g., certain boyhood gender disorders may have an endocrinologic component and sometimes correlate with later homosexuality. See Richard Friedman, *Male Homosexuality: A Contemporary Psychoanalytic Perspective* (New Haven: Yale Univ. Press, 1988).

11. See Richard Isay, *Being Homosexual: Gay Men and Their Development* (New York: Farrar, Straus, and Giroux, 1989), who takes this position but also claims that "the manner in which [this immutable-from-birth sexual orientation] is expressed appears to have multiple and diverse roots that may be profoundly influenced by a variety of early experience" (21). Friedman, *Male Homosexuality*, holds the tentative position that some aspects of homosexual object choice are for some people constitutional.

12. Adrienne Rich, "Compulsory Heterosexuality and Lesbian Existence," *Signs* 5 (1980): 631-60; and Carla Golden, "Diversity and Variability in Women's Sexual Identities," in *Lesbian Psychologies*, ed. Boston Lesbian Psychologies Collective (Urbana and Chicago: Univ. of Illinois Press, 1987), 19-34. For a more extended discussion of varieties of lesbianism, see Arlene Stein, "Sisters and Queers: The Decentering of Lesbian Feminism," *Socialist Review* 22 (1992): 33-55, and "Sexuality, Generation and the Self: Constructions of Lesbian Identity in the 'Decisive' Generation," Ph.D. diss., University of California, Berkeley, 1992.

13. Sociologist Robert Connell, in *Gender and Power* (Stanford: Stanford Univ. Press, 1987), 209, points to the systematic layering of masculinity and femininity in the personality, such that normally the surface personality that is compatible with social role is constructed by the repression of its opposite. I adapt his point here. I do not even begin to consider the fact that there are many homosexualities and many heterosexualities, all of which include and repress each other.

14. On Freud's teleology, see Nancy Chodorow, *The Reproduction of Mothering* (Berkeley and Los Angeles: Univ. of California Press, 1978), chap. 9; and Roy Schafer, "Problems in Freud's Psychology of Women," *Journal of the American Psychoanalytic Association* 22 (1974): 459-85.

15. Jessica Benjamin, in "Father and Daughter: Identification with Difference—A Contribution to Gender Heterodoxy," *Psychoanalytic Dialogues* 1 (1991): 277-99, and "Identificatory Love and Gender Development," in Anthony Elliot and Stephen

Frosh, eds., *Psychoanalysis in Contexts: Paths between Theory and Modern Culture* (New York and London: Routledge, forthcoming) develops the concept of identificatory love in a boy's attachment to his father.

16. Lewes, *Psychoanalytic Theory*, 82, 86.

17. See Stoller, *Perversion: The Erotic Form of Hatred* (New York: Pantheon, 1975), Stoller, *Sexual Excitement* (New York: Pantheon, 1979); Stoller, *Observing the Erotic Imagination*; Person, *Dreams of Love*; and Joyce McDougall, *Theatres of the Mind: Illusion and Truth on the Psychoanalytic Stage* (London: Free Association Books, 1986).

18. See, e.g., Marjorie R. Leonard, "Fathers and Daughters: The Significance of 'Fathering' in the Psychosexual Development of the Girl," *International Journal of Psycho-Analysis* 47 (1966): 325-34; and Janine Chasseguet-Smirgel, "Freud and Female Sexuality: The Consideration of Some Blind Spots in the Exploration of the 'Dark Continent,'" in *Sexuality and Mind* (New York: New York Univ. Press, 1986), 9-28.

19. Freud, *Three Essays on the Theory of Sexuality*; Phyllis Greenacre, "Perversions: General Considerations regarding Their Genetic and Dynamic Background," *Psychoanalytic Study of the Child* 23 (1968): 47-62; Janine Chasseguet-Smirgel, *Creativity and Perversion* (London: Free Association Books, 1985); Stoller, *Perversion*, *Sexual Excitement*, and *Observing the Erotic Imagination*; McDougall, *Theatres of the Mind*; Robert D. Stolorow and Frank M. Lachman, *Psychoanalysis of Developmental Arrests* (New York: International Univ. Press, 1980); Charles Socarides, *Homosexuality* (New York: Aronson, 1978); Charles Socarides, "A Unitary Theory of Sexual Perversions," in Thomas Karasu and Charles Socarides, eds., *On Sexuality* (New York: International Univ. Press, 1979), 161-88; Charles Socarides, *The Preoedipal Origin and Psychoanalytic Therapy of Sexual Perversions* (New York: International Univ. Press, 1988); and Joyce McDougall, "Homosexuality in Women," in Janine Chasseguet-Smirgel, ed., *Female Sexuality: New Psychoanalytic Views* (Ann Arbor: Univ. of Michigan Press, 1970), 171-212.

20. Kernberg, in "Barriers," 195, notes the "intense envy and hatred of women in many male patients," an observation which begins with Karen Horney, in "The Flight from Womanhood" and "The Dread of Women," and with Melanie Klein,

in "The Early Stages of the Oedipus Complex" and other writings. See also Slater, *Glory of Hera*.

21. See Eleanor Maccoby and Carol Jacklin, *The Psychology of Sex Differences* (Stanford: Stanford Univ. Press, 1974); and Miriam Johnson, *Strong Mothers, Weak Wives* (Berkeley and Los Angeles: Univ. of California Press, 1988).

22. Fritz Morgenthaler, *Homosexuality, Heterosexuality, Perversion* (New York: Analytic Press, 1988).

23. See Hershey, "On a Type of Heterosexuality," and Ethel S. Person, "The Omni-Available Woman and Lesbian Sex: Two Fantasy Themes and Their Relationship to the Male Developmental Experience," in Gerald I. Fogel, Frederick M. Lane, and Robert S. Liebert, eds., *The Psychology of Men* (New York: Basic Books, 1986), 71-94. For an earlier contribution, see Annie Reich, "Narcissistic Object Choice in Women," *Journal of the American Psychoanalytic Association* 1 (1953): 22-44.

24. Kirkpatrick is cited in "Toward Further Understanding of Homosexual Women," Abby Wolfson, reporter, *Journal of the American Psychoanalytic Association* 35 (1987): 169.

25. M. Balint, "Perversions and Genitality," 136, 142.

26. In the case of Balint, such a critique would, I believe, read contemporary discourse and politics into an earlier era.

27. McDougall, *Theatres of the Mind*, 256, 280.

28. Kernberg, "Aggression and Love" and "Sadomasochism."

29. Stoller, *Observing the Erotic Imagination*, vii-viii, 7.

30. Ibid., vii, 97.

31. Person, *Dreams of Love*, 347.

32. Stoller, *Observing the Erotic Imagination*, 9, 184.

33. Person, *Dreams of Love*, 339.

34. Kernberg, "Boundaries and Structures," 278-79, 293. See also, e.g., Kernberg, "Barriers."

35. Kernberg, "Boundaries and Structures," 297.

36. Kernberg, "Mature Love," 227-28.

37. Ibid., 217.

38. Kernberg, "Boundaries and Structures," 279, 278, and "Barriers," 212.

39. Kernberg, "Boundaries and Structures," 299.

40. Kernberg, "Mature Love," 220-21.

41. Person, *Dreams of Love*, 14.

42. Ibid., 286. Person is noting here that love doesn't have to be heterosexual to involve difference. But if people indeed choose opposite-gender partners because erotic passion and love thrive on difference, we should be surprised by the extensive age, class, race, and religious endogamy still present in our society. I also note that although homosexual object choice may often cross these other categories of difference—perhaps to enhance the excitement that comes from difference in a case of same-gender choice—accounts of problems in lesbian object choice point rather to similarity bordering on merging. See Susan Krieger, *The Mirror Dance* (Philadelphia: Temple Univ. Press, 1983); and Joyce P. Lindenbaum, "The Shattering of an Illusion: The Problem of Competition in Lesbian Relationships," *Feminist Studies* 11 (1985): 85-103.

43. It may in fact be appropriate to center an account of romantic passion in our society on heterosexual passion, since that is what most people experience or dream about and what our cultural categories offer us. It is, rather, Person's normative developmental theory that I address here.

44. Person, *Dreams of Love*, 93, 100.

45. Jessica Benjamin, in *Bonds of Love* and "Father and Daughter," describes and theorizes the development of "identificatory love," which certainly combines erotism and identification. She postulates that such identificatory love characterizes both children's relationship to and desire for the father during the rapprochement subphase, and that both have a sort of longing to be separate through the father and to feel for themselves the desire and agency that they sense the father has. Desire is thereby symbolized, as in French psychoanalytic theory, by the phallus. Benjamin's account describes powerfully how heterosexual love can go wrong for boy and girl in this process and how the girl tends to get submission and alienation, rather than desire, from her father, but it is not meant to explain why children of either sex become psychologically or erotically heterosexual. See Benjamin, *The Bonds of Love: Psychoanalysis, Feminism, and the Problem of Domination* (New York: Pantheon, 1988), and "Father and Daughter."

46. Chasseguet-Smirgel, *Creativity and Perversion*, 4, 6, 12.

47. McDougall, *Theatres of the Mind*, 248-49, 267-68.

48. Jacques Lacan, *Feminine Sexuality*, Juliet Mitchell and Jacqueline Rose, eds. (New York: Norton, 1982).

49. Kernberg, "Mature Love," 268, and "Boundaries and Structures," 284, 285.

50. Person, *Dreams of Love*, 265.

51. I am indebted for this double conceptualization to R.W. Connell, who points out that psychoanalytic sociologies and culture and personality studies have tended to see culture and society as in some sense *resultants* of prevalent psychological tendencies and conflicts. In the case of gender and sexuality, he suggests, the reverse is also true: "The power relations of the society become a constitutive principle of personality dynamics through being adopted as a personal project" (*Gender and Power*, 215). Institutions, practices, cultural productions, and inegalitarian social relations inform and help to constitute masculinities and femininities and the forms of sexuality.

52. For a classic statement, see Gayle Rubin, "The Traffic in Women: Notes on a 'Political Economy' of Sex," in Rayna Reiter, ed., *Toward an Anthropology of Women* (New York: Monthly Review Press, 1975), 157-210. More recently, see Judith Butler, *Gender Trouble: Feminism and Subversion of Identity* in Linda J. Nicholson, ed., *Feminism/Postmodernism* (New York: Routledge, 1990), 324-40. Many other feminist writers criticize heterosexuality; I cite here two that specifically challenge the normative psychoanalytic story.

53. Benjamin, *Bonds of Love*; Susan Contratto, "Father Presence in Women's Psychological Development," in Gerald M. Platt, Jerome Rabow, and Marion Goldman, eds., *Advances in Psychoanalytic Sociology* (Malabar, Fla.: Krieger, 1987), 138-57.

54. On the early genital phase, see Herman Roiphe and Eleanor Galenson, *Infantile Origins of Sexual Identity* (New York: International Univ. Press, 1981). On girls' depressive affect during the rapprochement crisis, see Margaret S. Mahler, Fred Pine, and Anni Bergman, *The Psychological Birth of the Human Infant* (New York: Basic Books, 1975).

55. Benjamin, *Bonds of Love*, 106.

56. Contratto, "Father Presence in Women's Psychological Development," 143, 144, 148.

57. On fathers' treatment of boys and girls, see Miriam Johnson, "Fathers, Mothers, and Sex-Typing," *Sociological In-*

quiry 45 (1975): 15-26; Johnson, *Strong Mothers, Weak Wives*; Patricia K. Kerig, Philip A. Cowan, and Carolyn Pape Cowan, "Marital Quality and Gender Differences in Parent-Child Interaction," *Developmental Psychology* 29 (1993): 931-39; and Cowan, Cowan, and Kerig, "Mothers, Fathers, Sons, and Daughters: Gender Differences in Family Formation and Parenting Style," in Philip A. Cowan et al., eds., *Family, Self, and Society: Toward a New Agenda for Family Research* (Hillsdale, N.J.: Erlbaum, 1993), 165-95. See also chapter 3 for further discussion.

58. Johnson, *Strong Mothers, Weak Wives*.

59. See also Annie Reich, "Narcissistic Object Choice in Women."

60. Contratto, "Father Presence in Women's Psychological Development," 152.

61. As I noted earlier, this theme is found in psychoanalytic writings since Horney's "Dread of Women." See also Alice Balint, "Love for the Mother and Mother-Love"; Chasseguet-Smirgel, "Freud and Female Sexuality"; Chodorow, *Reproduction of Mothering*; Susan Contratto (Weisskopf), "Maternal Sexuality and Asexual Motherhood," *Signs* 5 (1980): 766-82; and Chodorow and Contratto, "The Fantasy of the Perfect Mother," in *Feminism and Psychoanalytic Theory*, 79-96.

Recently, Contratto has written about an unhappy twist in the relations between the stance of the infant toward the mother and this denial of maternal subjectivity ("The Illusive Father—Everywhere/Nowhere: A Reply to the Notion of the Uninvolved Mother in Father-Daughter Incest," paper presented at the Meetings of the American Psychological Association, Washington, D.C., Aug. 1992). In the case of father-daughter incest, she notes, patients (and therapists) often assume that the mother knew and may even pay more attention to betrayal by the mother than to the commission of incest by the father. Contratto suggests that as such traumatic experiences lead to fragmentation and regression, infantile beliefs in the omnipotent mother are resurrected; it is the omnipotent mother of infancy who is assumed to know all.

62. As a social scientist trained to assume the basic cultural and social constructedness of all gendered and sexual experience and categories, including our understandings of biology, I have noticed the ease with which psychoanalysts turn to "real" biological functions and anatomy in the case of gender

and sexuality. It has occurred to me that training, in addition to Freud's similar inclinations, has a role in their case. Such functions and anatomy were first introduced in the medical context, where they joined a panoply of taken-for-granted cultural assumptions about the naturalness of gender. By contrast, notions about conflict, psychic structure, unconscious mental functioning, and so forth are introduced only in the more exclusively psychoanalytic-psychodynamic context, with much less cultural or medical baggage.

63. I am grateful to Frann Michel for first pointing out this inconsistency to me, in an early version of her dissertation chapter "William Faulkner as a Lesbian Author" (in Michel, "After the World Broke: Cross-Gender Representation in Works by Willa Cather, William Faulkner, and Djuna Barnes," Ph.D. diss., University of California, Berkeley, 1990).

Lewes points out that a pejorative psychoanalytic theory and discriminatory organizational practice have themselves prevented homosexuals, as practitioners, from contributing to the creation of a theory of their own functioning. Historically, women's entrance into the field was essential to allowing a view of women as different rather than inferior, as well as a view of a differentiated and complex femininity with both advantages and problems. Lewes links these two discourses, paralleling the traditional psychoanalytic theory of homosexuality with the theory of female psychology: homosexuals identify with their mother, make narcissistic object choices, are convinced of their own castration, choose sexual objects in order to gain a penis, attempt to be loved instead of to love, and have flawed superegos and other ego deficits. The "gynecophobia" of the early theory of female development—which was challenged especially by female analysts—now characterizes the view of homosexuality. As analysts saw only the disturbed homosexuals who came for treatment, they concluded that all homosexuals were disturbed, whereas their treatment of neurotic heterosexuals did not lead to the presumption that heterosexuality was a disorder (Lewes, *Psychoanalytic Theory*, 231-39). In recent years these issues have reached the center of organized American psychoanalysis, as a vociferous minority tries to prevent the training and promotion to training analyst of gays and lesbians.

64. McDougall, *Theatres of the Mind*, 247.

65. Gabriel García Marquez, *Love in the Time of Cholera* (New York: Knopf, 1988).

66. Person, "The Omni-Available Woman," 74, reports that "male fantasies are frequently impersonal; autonomy, control, and physical prowess are central concerns. . . . Male fantasies of rape, mastery, transgression, and bondage are widespread. . . . domination is unquestionably a primary motif." The Fantasy Project at the Columbia Psychoanalytic Center for Training and Research, she goes on to note, found that 11 percent of the men studied had fantasied torturing a partner, 20 percent had fantasied whipping or beating, and 44 percent had fantasied forcing a partner to submit to sex, whereas "comparable figures for women are 0 percent, 1 percent and 10 percent."

67. See, e.g., McDougall, "Homosexuality in Women"; Socarides, *Homosexuality*, "A Unitary Theory," and *Preoedipal Origin*; and Stolorow and Lachman, *Psychoanalysis of Developmental Arrests*.

68. This point is made in Steven Epstein, "Sexuality and Identity: The Contribution of Object-Relations Theory to a Constructionist Sociology," *Theory and Society* 20 (1991): 825-73. Such an account also tends to locate the origins of the pathology in disturbances in the relation to the mother, since the father is traditionally not seen as important until the oedipal period.

69. Kernberg, "Barriers" and "Boundaries and Structures."

70. I mean to imply not that psychoanalysts are necessarily heterosexual but only that activism and theory take place in both psychoanalytic and political-sexual-societal arenas.

3. Individuality and Difference in How Women and Men Love

1. See, e.g., Golden, "Diversity and Variability"; Arlene Stein, "Sisters and Queers"; Katz, *Gay/Lesbian Almanac*; and Martin B. Duberman, Martha Vicinus, and George Chauncey, Jr., eds., *Hidden from History: Reclaiming the Gay and Lesbian Past* (New York: New American Library, 1989), among many writings. Among psychoanalytic writings, one has only to look at any number of case studies of "perversion" (which is not to

ignore the kinds of generalizations about homosexuality and perversion discussed in chapter 2).

2. I note, though I cannot solve, a problem or limitation: love is particularly difficult to study clinically because, although the clinical situation is a two-person experience, and we can study love directly through the transference and countertransference as well as indirectly through our patients' descriptions of their lives, it is nonetheless the case that, as we describe how men and women love, we do so from the point of view of one person, and not with a double lens that sees fully from the point of view of both parties to the love relationship at the same time. Inevitably, the love partner in all our case descriptions and generalizations—unless we describe our countertransference feelings and fantasies as fully as we describe the transference feelings and fantasies of our patients— remains more object than subject, and the love relationship described does not exhibit the mutually constructed tensions, strengths, shifts, and fantasies that characterize any intense two-person relationship.

3. I have found that my (decades-removed) training as a psychological anthropologist, along with an ongoing interest in cross-cultural matters, has been invaluable in my work with non-Euro-American patients (as well as in problematizing Euro-American culture and the psychological universalisms that have emerged from its theorists). I have both a continuing sense of how vastly different psychological and familial practices and patterns are, cross-culturally, and some (albeit soberingly limited) concrete knowledge about a variety of non-Western cultures.

4. See Denis de Rougemont, *Love in the Western World* (New York: Pantheon, 1956); Gaylin and Person, *Passionate Attachments*; Carroll Smith-Rosenberg, *Disorderly Conduct: Visions of Gender in Victorian America* (Oxford and New York: Oxford Univ. Press, 1985), 9-76; Katz, "Invention of Heterosexuality"; Duberman, Vicinus, and Chauncey, *Hidden from History*; and Judith Plaskow, *Standing Again at Sinai* (New York: HarperCollins, 1990), 170-210. Particularly interesting cross-cultural studies include Thomas Gregor, *Anxious Pleasures: The Sexual Lives of an Amazonian People* (Chicago: Univ. of Chicago Press, 1985); Robert I. Levy, *Tahitians: Mind and Expe-*

rience in the Society Islands (Chicago: Univ. of Chicago Press, 1973), and Gilbert Herdt, *Guardians of the Flutes: Idioms of Masculinity* (New York: McGraw Hill, 1981).

5. Daphne du Maurier, *Rebecca* (New York: Doubleday, 1948); Philip Roth, *Portnoy's Complaint* (New York: Random House, 1983). For a remarkable discussion of such masculine fantasies in Shakespeare, see Janet Adelman, *Suffocating Mothers: Fantasies of Maternal Origin in Shakespeare's Plays*, Hamlet *to* The Tempest (New York: Routledge, 1992).

6. Irene Fast, *Gender Identity: A Differentiation Model* (Hillsdale, N.J.: Erlbaum, 1984), develops the distinction of subjective and objective gender: "Subjective definitions of masculinity and femininity must be distinguished from objective ones. Objectively defined, individuals' characteristics are masculine or feminine to the extent that they are typical of one or the other sex in a particular social group. Subjective definitions refer to personal constructs of masculinity and femininity, individuals' own notions, applied to themselves and to others, of what it is to be masculine and feminine" (77). So, for example, a woman's Rebecca fantasy may be intertwined with her sense of womanliness or femininity, but we might also say that Rebecca fantasies are more likely to characterize women than men.

7. Chasseguet-Smirgel, *Creativity and Perversion*, 12; McDougall, *Theatres of the Mind*, 267-68. See also Kernberg, "Boundaries and Structures," 284.

8. See, e.g., Hélène Cixous, "The Laugh of the Medusa," *Signs* 1 (1976): 875-93; and Luce Irigaray, *This Sex Which Is Not One* (Ithaca: Cornell Univ. Press, 1985).

9. Espín, "Cultural and Historical Influences on Sexuality in Hispanic/Latin Women: Implications for Psychotherapy," in Carol Vance, ed., *Pleasure and Danger: Exploring Female Sexuality* (New York: Monthly Review Press, 1984), 149-64; Moraga, "From a Long Line of Vendidas: Chicanas and Feminism," in Teresa de Lauretis, ed., *Feminist Studies/Critical Studies* (Madison: Univ. of Wisconsin Press, 1986), 173-90.

10. See Denise Kandiyoti, "Bargaining with Patriarchy," *Gender and Society* 2 (1988): 274-90. See also, on Morocco, Fatima Mernissi, *Beyond the Veil: Male-Female Dynamics in a Modern Muslim Society* (Cambridge: Schenkman, 1975); and,

on Italy, Anne Parsons, *Belief, Magic and Anomie* (New York: Free Press, 1969).

11. Nancy Cott, "Passionlessness: An Interpretation of Victorian Sexual Ideology," *Signs* 4 (1978): 219-36; Moraga, "From a Long Line of Vendidas."

12. Gloria Joseph, "Black Mothers and Daughters: Their Roles and Functions in American Society," in Joseph and Jill Lewis, *Common Differences* (Boston: South End Press, 1981, 75-126.

13. See Hazel Carby, "On the Threshold of the Woman's Era: Lynching, Empire, and Sexuality in Black Feminist Theory," *Critical Inquiry* 12 (1985): 262-77; and Patricia Hill Collins, *Black Feminist Thought: Knowledge, Consciousness and the Politics of Empowerment* (Boston: Unwin Hyman, 1990).

14. See Carby, "It Jus Be's Dat Way Sometime: The Sexual Politics of Women's Blues," *Radical America* 20 (1987): 9-22.

15. Connell, *Gender and Power*, 183-88; Tomás Almaguer, "Chicano Men: A Cartography of Homosexual Identity and Behavior," *Differences* 3 (1991): 75-100.

16. A longitudinal study of college graduates from the late 1950s—women caught between the old 1950s pattern emphasizing home and family and the emerging 1960s pattern of college graduate women having careers—compares women who followed a "feminine social clock" and those who followed a "masculine occupational clock"; see Ravenna Helson, Valerie Mitchell, and Geraldine Moane, "Personality and Patterns of Adherence and Nonadherence to the Social Clock," *Journal of Personality and Social Psychology* 46 (1984): 1079-96. This role comparison does not directly predict or mirror personality and unconscious femininity, but it indicates that comparable psychodynamics might exist.

17. See Chodorow, *Reproduction of Mothering* and *Feminism and Psychoanalytic Theory*.

18. See, e.g., Norma Alarcón, "What Kind of a Lover Have You Made Me, Mother: Towards a Theory of Chicanas' Feminism and Cultural Identity through Poetry," in Audrey T. McCluskey, ed., *Perspectives on Feminism and Identity in Women of Color* (Bloomington: Indiana Univ. Press, 1985), 85-110; Terri Apter, *Altered Loves: Mothers and Daughters during Adolescence* (New York: Ballantine, 1990); Myrtha Chabran, "Exiles" in

Carol Ascher, Louise DeSalvo, and Sara Ruddick, eds., *Between Women: Biographers, Novelists, Critics, Teachers and Artists Write about Their Work on Women* (Boston: Beacon Press, 1984), 161-69; Bell Gayle Chevigny, "Daughters Writing: Toward a Theory of Women's Biography," in *Between Women*, 357-79; Patricia Hill Collins, "The Meaning of Motherhood in Black Culture and Black Mother-Daughter Relationships," *Sage* 4 (1987): 3-10; Akemi Kikumura, *Through Harsh Winters: The Life of a Japanese Immigrant Woman* (Novato, Cal.: Chandler and Sharpe, 1981); Moraga, "From a Long Line of Vendidas"; Alice Walker, "In Search of Our Mothers' Gardens," in Sara Ruddick and Pamela Daniels, eds., *Working It Out* (New York: Pantheon, 1977), 93-102. Within fiction by women of different racial-ethnic groups, see Virginia Woolf's *To the Lighthouse*, Amy Tan's *The Joy Luck Club* (New York: G.P. Putnam's Sons, 1989), and Jamaica Kincaid's *Annie John* (New York: Farrar, Straus & Giroux, 1983, 1984, 1985) and *Lucy* (New York: Farrar, Straus & Giroux, 1990).

I have been previously misread to be claiming a universal, idealized, usually preoedipally constructed mother-daughter attachment, but when I say "love," this is not what I mean or what I described in *Reproduction of Mothering*. I mean an intense, passionate attachment, which might include or be at war with envy, hatred, ambivalence. We know from psychoanalysis that intense emotions always come with their opposite. Nor do I mean that this is *all* that matters to a daughter, but it does matter enormously.

19. I believe that we do not know nearly enough about how romantic and sexual desires are formed during adolescence—when there is a coming together of childhood, culture, and pubertal development—and that as we learn more, we will find this period crucial. Martin's research on adolescent girls' and boys' senses of sexual self ("Puberty, Sexuality, and the Self") confirms this claim.

20. See Benjamin, *Bonds of Love*; Daphne de Marneffe, "Toddlers' Understandings of Gender," Ph.D. diss., University of California, Berkeley, 1993); and Roiphe and Galenson, *Infantile Origins of Sexual Identity*.

21. See Klein, "Early Stages of the Oedipus Conflict" and "Envy and Gratitude."

22. As long as we follow the Freudian tradition—as mainstream psychoanalysts as well as Lacanians and other French theorists since Freud have done—there is no other possible resolution of the overwhelming fear of the mother than this repudiation and installation of male dominant heterosexuality. Pro-female psychoanalysts such as Chasseguet-Smirgel, and even feminist theorists such as Benjamin, can only envision this turn to the father and symbolization of paternal and phallic power and desire as the solution for women as well as for men. (Benjamin emphasizes the daughter's need for accepted identificatory love in relation to her father as the solution to the potential alienation of her desire.)

In recently rereading Klein, it struck me that there could have been, psychoanalytically, another route. Klein describes clearly and forcefully the repudiation of feminine identifications and maternal dependency in both boys and girls as ingredient in the overvaluation of the penis, but in her work on early object relations she also makes reparation toward the mother in the depressive position into a central, perhaps *the* central, developmental goal. If Kleinians had attended to gender development and continued Klein's focus on gender differences in the Oedipus complex, it seems to me that a solution to the fear of femininity and the maternal breast in reparation toward the mother, rather than rejection of her, would have been an alternative developmental model. On male and female development, see Klein, "Early Stages of the Oedipus Conflict" and "Envy and Gratitude"; on reparation, see her writings in general, especially "A Contribution to the Psychogenesis of Manic-Depressive States" and "Love, Guilt and Reparation," in *Love, Guilt and Reparation*.

23. See Freud, "Special Type of Choice of Object" and "Universal Tendency to Debasement."

24. Adrienne Rich, *Of Woman Born: Motherhood as Experience and Institution* (New York: Norton, 1976), 257-59.

25. See Miriam Johnson, "Fathers, Mothers, and Sex-Typing" and *Strong Mothers, Weak Wives*; Kerig, Cowan, and Cowan, "Marital Quality and Gender Differences"; and Cowan, Cowan, and Kerig, "Mothers, Fathers, Sons, and Daughters."

26. See Mavis Hetherington, "Effects of Father Absence on

Personality Development in Adolescent Daughters," *Developmental Psychology* 7 (1972): 313-26.

27. See Sarah Elbert, "Introduction" to Louisa May Alcott, *Work* (New York: Schocken, 1977), ix-xliv, and Jean Strouse, *Alice James: A Biography* (New York: Bantam, 1980).

28. Chodorow, "Oedipal Asymmetries and Heterosexual Knots," in *Feminism and Psychoanalytic Theory*, 66-78.

29. Marilyn Frye, "The Possibility of Feminist Theory," in Deborah Rhode, ed., *Theoretical Perspectives on Sexual Difference* (New Haven: Yale Univ. Press, 1990), 180.

30. See, e.g., Virginia Goldner, "Toward a Critical Relational Theory of Gender," *Psychoanalytic Dialogues* 1 (1991): 249-72; and Barrie Thorne, *Gender Play: Girls and Boys in School* (New Brunswick: Rutgers Univ. Press, 1993).

References

Adelman, Janet. *Suffocating Mothers: Fantasies of Maternal Origin in Shakespeare's Plays*, Hamlet *to* The Tempest. New York: Routledge, 1992.

Alarcón, Norma. "What Kind of a Lover Have You Made Me, Mother: Towards a Theory of Chicanas' Feminism and Cultural Identity through Poetry." In *Perspectives on Feminism and Identity in Women of Color*, ed. Audrey T. McCluskey, pp. 85-110. Bloomington: Indiana Univ. Press, 1985.

Almaguer, Tomás. "Chicano Men: A Cartography of Homosexual Identity and Behavior." *Differences* 3 (1991): 75-100.

Apter, Terri. *Altered Loves: Mothers and Daughters during Adolescence*. New York: Ballantine, 1990.

Balint, Alice. "Love for the Mother and Mother-Love" (1939). In Michael Balint, *Primary Love and Psycho-Analytic Technique*, pp. 91-108. New York: Liveright, 1965.

Balint, Michael. "Eros and Aphrodite" (1936). In *Primary Love and Psycho-Analytic Technique*, pp. 59-73. New York: Liveright, 1965.

———. "On Genital Love" (1947). In *Primary Love*, pp. 109-20. *See* M. Balint, "Eros."

———. "Perversions and Genitality" (1956). In *Primary Love*, pp. 136-47. *See* M. Balint, "Eros."

Benjamin, Jessica. *The Bonds of Love: Psychoanalysis, Feminism, and the Problem of Domination*. New York: Pantheon, 1988.

———. "Father and Daughter: Identification with Difference—A Contribution to Gender Heterodoxy." *Psychoanalytic Dialogues* 1 (1991): 277-99.

———. "Identificatory Love and Gender Development." In *Psychoanalysis in Contexts: Paths between Theory and Modern*

Culture, ed. Anthony Elliott and Stephen Frosh. New York: Routledge, 1994.

Bernheimer, Charles, and Clair Kahane, eds. *In Dora's Case: Freud—Hysteria—Feminism*. New York: Columbia Univ. Press, 1985.

Bertin, Celia. *Marie Bonaparte*. New York: Harcourt Brace Jovanovich, 1982.

Bonaparte, Marie. *Female Sexuality*. New York: International Universities Press, 1953.

Breuer, Josef, and Sigmund Freud. *Studies on Hysteria* (1893-95). In *S.E.*, vol. 2. *See* Freud.

Brunswick, Ruth Mack. "The Preoedipal Phase of the Libido Development." In *The Psychoanalytic Reader*, ed. Robert Fliess, pp. 231-53. New York: International Universities Press, 1948.

Butler, Judith. *Gender Trouble: Feminism and the Subversion of Identity*. New York: Routledge, 1990.

Byne, William, and Bruce Parsons. "Human Sexual Orientation: The Biologic Theories Reappraised." *Archives of General Psychiatry* 50 (1993): 228-39.

Carby, Hazel. "'On the Threshold of the Woman's Era': Lynching, Empire, and Sexuality in Black Feminist Theory." *Critical Inquiry* 12 (1985): 262-77.

———. "It Jus Be's Dat Way Sometime: The Sexual Politics of Women's Blues." *Radical America* 20 (1987): 9-22.

Chabran, Myrtha. "Exiles." In *Between Women: Biographers, Novelists, Critics, Teachers and Artists Write about Their Work on Women*, ed. Carol Ascher, Louise DeSalvo, and Sara Ruddick, pp. 161-69. Boston: Beacon, 1984.

Chasseguet-Smirgel, Janine. "Freud and Female Sexuality: The Consideration of Some Blind Spots in the Exploration of the 'Dark Continent'" (1976). In *Sexuality and Mind*, pp. 9-28. New York: New York Univ. Press, 1986.

———. *Creativity and Perversion*. London: Free Association Books, 1985.

Chevigny, Bell Gale. "Daughters Writing: Toward a Theory of Women's Biography." In *Between Women*, pp. 357-79. *See* Chabran.

Chodorow, Nancy J. "Oedipal Asymmetries and Heterosexual Knots" (1976), In *Feminism and Psychoanalytic Theory*, pp. 66-78. *See* Chodorow, *Feminism*.

———. *The Reproduction of Mothering*. Berkeley: Univ. of California Press, 1978.

———. *Feminism and Psychoanalytic Theory*. New Haven: Yale Univ. Press; Cambridge: Polity Press, 1989.

———. "Psychoanalytic Feminism and the Psychoanalytic Psychology of Women." In *Feminism and Psychoanalytic Theory*, pp. 178-98. *See* Chodorow, *Feminism*.

———. "Seventies Questions for Thirties Women." In *Feminism and Psychoanalytic Theory*, pp. 199-218. *See* Chodorow, *Feminism*.

———. "Where Have All the Eminent Women Psychoanalysts Gone? Like the Bubbles in Champagne, They Rose to the Top and Disappeared." In *Social Roles and Social Institutions: Essays in Honor of Rose Laub Coser*, ed. Judith R. Blau and Norman Goodman, pp. 167-94. Boulder, Colo.: Westview, 1991.

———, and Susan Contratto. "The Fantasy of the Perfect Mother" (1981). In *Feminism and Psychoanalytic Theory*. pp. 79-96. *See* Chodorow, *Feminism*.

Cixous, Hélène. "The Laugh of the Medusa." *Signs* 1 (1976): 875-93.

Collins, Patricia Hill. "The Meaning of Motherhood in Black Culture and Black Mother-Daughter Relationships." *Sage* 4 (1987): 3-10.

———. *Black Feminist Thought: Knowledge, Consciousness, and the Politics of Empowerment*. Boston: Unwin Hyman, 1990.

Connell, Robert W. *Gender and Power*. Stanford, Calif.: Stanford Univ. Press, 1987.

Contratto [Weisskopf], Susan. "Maternal Sexuality and Asexual Motherhood." *Signs* 5 (1980): 766-82.

———. "Father Presence in Women's Psychological Development." In *Advances in Psychoanalytic Sociology*, ed. Gerald M. Platt, Jerome Rabow, and Marion Goldman, pp. 138-57. Malabar, Fla.: Krieger, 1987.

———. "The Illusive Father—Everywhere/Nowhere: A Reply to the Notion of the Uninvolved Mother in Father-Daughter Incest." Paper presented at the Meetings of the American Psychological Association, Washington, D.C., August 1992.

Cott, Nancy. "Passionlessness: An Interpretation of Victorian Sexual Ideology, 1750-1850." *Signs* 4 (1978): 219-36.

Cowan, Philip A., Carolyn P. Cowan, and Patricia Kerig. "Mothers, Fathers, Sons and Daughters: Gender Differences in Family Formation and Parenting Style." In *Family, Self, and Society*, ed. Philip A. Cowan, Dorothy Field, Donald A. Hansen, Arlene Skolnick, and Guy E. Swanson, pp. 165-95. Hillsdale, N.J.: Lawrence Erlbaum, 1993.

Decker, Hannah S. "The Choice of a Name: 'Dora' and Freud's Relationship with Breuer." *Journal of the American Psychoanalytic Association* 30 (1982): 113-36.

―――. *Freud, Dora, and Vienna 1900*. New York: Free Press, 1990.

de Marneffe, Daphne. "Looking and Listening: The Construction of Clinical Knowledge in Charcot and Freud." *Signs* 17 (1991): 71-111.

―――. "Toddlers' Understandings of Gender." Ph.D. diss., Univ. of California, Berkeley, 1993.

de Rougemont, Denis. *Love in the Western World*. New York: Pantheon, 1956.

Deutsch, Helene. *The Psychology of Women*. Vol. 1, *Girlhood*. New York: Grune & Stratton, 1944.

―――. *Confrontations with Myself*. New York: Norton, 1973.

Duberman, Martin B., Martha Vicinus, and George Chauncey, Jr., eds. *Hidden from History: Reclaiming the Gay and Lesbian Past*. New York: New American Library, 1989.

Du Maurier, Daphne. *Rebecca*. New York: Doubleday, 1948.

Elbert, Sarah. "Introduction" to Louisa May Alcott, *Work*, pp. ix-xliv. New York: Schocken, 1977.

Epstein, Steven. "Sexuality and Identity: The Contribution of Object-Relations Theory to a Constructionist Sociology." *Theory and Society* 20 (1991): 825-73.

Erikson, Erik H. "Reality and Actuality: An Address." In *In Dora's Case*, pp. 44-55. *See* Bernheimer and Kahane.

Espín, Oliva. "Cultural and Historical Influences on Sexuality in Hispanic/Latin Women: Implications for Psychotherapy." In *Pleasure and Danger: Exploring Female Sexuality*, ed. Carol Vance, pp. 149-64. New York: Monthly Review Press, 1984.

Fast, Irene. *Gender Identity: A Differentiation Model*. Hillsdale, N.J.: Lawrence Erlbaum, 1984.

Felman, Shoshana. "Rereading Femininity." *Yale French Studies* 62 (1981): 19-44.

Foley, Helene P., ed. *The Homeric Hymn to Demeter: Translation, Commentary, and Interpretive Essays*. Princeton, N.J.: Princeton Univ. Press, 1993.

Foucault, Michel. *The History of Sexuality*. Vol. 1, *An Introduction*. New York: Pantheon, 1978.

Freud, Sigmund. *The Interpretation of Dreams* (1900). In *Standard Edition of the Complete Psychological Works of Sigmund Freud*, ed. James Strachey [S.E.], vol. 4. London: Hogarth Press, 1953-74.

———. *Fragment of an Analysis of a Case of Hysteria* ["Dora"] (1905) *S.E.*, 7:3-122.

———. *Three Essays on the Theory of Sexuality* (1905). *S.E.*, 7:125-243.

———. "'Civilized' Sexual Morality and Modern Nervous Illness" (1908). *S.E.*, 9:177-204.

———. *Notes upon a Case of Obsessional Neurosis* ["the Rat Man"] (1909). *S.E.*, 10:153-318.

———. "A Special Type of Choice of Object Made by Men (Contributions to the Psychology of Love, I)" (1910). *S.E.*, 11:163-75.

———. "On the Universal Tendency to Debasement in the Sphere of Love (Contributions to the Psychology of Love, II)" (1912). *S.E.*, 11:177-90.

———. "The Dynamics of Transference" (1912). *S.E.*, 12:97-108.

———. "On Narcissism: An Introduction" (1914). *S.E.*, 14:67-102.

———. *Introductory Lectures on Psycho-Analysis* (1916-17). *S.E.*, vols. 15-16.

———. "Mourning and Melancholia" (1917). *S.E.*, 14:237-58.

———. *From the History of an Infantile Neurosis* ["the Wolf Man"] (1918). *S.E.*, 17:3-122.

———. "The Taboo of Virginity (Contributions to the Psychology of Love, III)" (1918). *S.E.*, 11:191-208.

———. "'A Child Is Being Beaten': A Contribution to the Study of the Origin of Sexual Perversions" (1919). *S.E.*, 17:175-204.

———. "The Psychogenesis of a Case of Homosexuality in a Woman" (1920). *S.E.*, 18:145-72.

————. "The Dissolution of the Oedipus Complex" (1924). *S.E.*, 19:173-79.

————. "Some Psychical Consequences of the Anatomical Distinction between the Sexes" (1925). *S.E.*, 19:248-58.

————. "Fetishism" (1927). *S.E.*, 21:149-57.

————. *Civilization and Its Discontents* (1930). *S.E.*, 21:59-145.

————. "Female Sexuality" (1931). *S.E.*, 21:225-43.

————. "Femininity" (1933). In *New Introductory Lectures on Psycho-Analysis* (1933). *S.E.*, 22: 112-35.

————. "Analysis Terminable and Interminable" (1937). *S.E.*, 23:209-53.

————. "Medusa's Head" (1940). *S.E.*, 18:273-74.

Friedman, Richard. *Male Homosexuality: A Contemporary Psychoanalytic Perspective.* New Haven: Yale Univ. Press, 1988.

Frye, Marilyn. "The Possibility of Feminist Theory." In *Theoretical Perspectives on Sexual Difference*, ed. Deborah Rhode, pp. 174-84. New Haven: Yale Univ. Press, 1990.

Gallop, Jane. "Keys to Dora." In *In Dora's Case*, pp. 200-220. *See* Bernheimer and Kahane.

García Marquez, Gabriel. *Love in the Time of Cholera.* New York: Knopf, 1988.

Gaylin, Willard, and Ethel Person, eds. *Passionate Attachments: Thinking about Love.* New York: Free Press, 1988.

Golden, Carla. "Diversity and Variability in Women's Sexual Identities." In *Lesbian Psychologies*, ed. Boston Lesbian Psychologies Collective, pp. 19-34. Urbana: Univ. of Illinois Press, 1987.

Goldner, Virginia. "Toward a Critical Relational Theory of Gender." *Psychoanalytic Dialogues* 1 (1991): 249-72.

Greenacre, Phyllis. "Perversions: General Considerations regarding Their Genetic and Dynamic Background." *Psychoanalytic Study of the Child* 23 (1968): 47-62.

Gregor, Thomas. *Anxious Pleasures: The Sexual Lives of an Amazonian People.* Chicago: Univ. of Chicago Press, 1985.

Grosskurth, Phyllis. *Melanie Klein: Her World and Her Work.* New York: Knopf, 1986.

Helson, Ravenna, Valerie Mitchell, and Geraldine Moane. "Personality and Patterns of Adherence and Nonadherence to the Social Clock." *Journal of Personality and Social Psychology* 46 (1984): 1079-96.

Herdt, Gilbert. *Guardians of the Flutes: Idioms of Masculinity*. New York: McGraw-Hill, 1981.

Hershey, David W. "On a Type of Heterosexuality, and the Fluidity of Object Relations." *Journal of the American Psychoanalytic Association.* 37 (1989): 147-71.

Hetherington, Mavis. "Effects of Father Absence on Personality Development in Adolescent Daughters." *Developmental Psychology* 7 (1972): 313-26.

Horney, Karen. "The Flight from Womanhood: The Masculinity Complex in Women as Viewed by Men and by Women" (1926). In *Feminine Psychology*, pp. 54-70, New York: Norton, 1967.

———. "The Dread of Women" (1932). In *Feminine Psychology*, pp. 133-46. *See* Horney, "Flight."

Irigaray, Luce. *This Sex Which Is Not One*. Ithaca, N.Y.: Cornell Univ. Press, 1985.

Isay, Richard. *Being Homosexual: Gay Men and Their Development*. New York: Farrar, Straus & Giroux, 1989.

Johnson, Miriam. "Fathers, Mothers, and Sex-Typing." *Sociological Inquiry* 45 (1975): 15-26.

———. *Strong Mothers, Weak Wives*. Berkeley: Univ. of California Press, 1988.

Joseph, Gloria. "Black Mothers and Daughters: Their Roles and Functions in American Society." In *Common Differences*, ed. Joseph and Jill Lewis, pp. 75-126. Boston: South End Press, 1981.

Jung, Carl J., and Karoly Kerenyi. *Essays on a Science of Mythology: The Myth of the Divine Child and the Mysteries of Eleusis*. Princeton, N.J.: Princeton Univ. Press, 1963.

Kandiyoti, Denise. "Bargaining with Patriarchy." *Gender and Society* 2 (1988): 274-90.

Katz, Jonathan N. *The Gay/Lesbian Almanac*. New York: Harper & Row, 1983.

———. "The Invention of Heterosexuality." *Socialist Review* 20 (1990): 7-34.

Kerig, Patricia, Philip A. Cowan and Carolyn Pape Cowan. "Marital Quality and Gender Differences in Parent-Child Interaction." *Developmental Psychology*, 29 (1993): 931-39.

Kernberg, Otto. "Barriers to Falling and Remaining in Love." In *Object Relations Theory and Clinical Psycho-Analysis*, pp. 185-213. New York: Jason Aronson, 1976.

———. "Mature Love: Prerequisites and Characteristics." In *Object Relations Theory*, pp. 215-39. *See* Kernberg, "Barriers."

———. "Boundaries and Structures in Love Relations." In *Internal World and External Reality*, pp. 277-305. New York: Jason Aronson, 1980.

———. "Between Conventionality and Aggression: The Boundaries of Passion." In *Passionate Attachments*, pp. 63-83. *See* Gaylin and Person.

———. "Aggression and Love in the Relationship of the Couple." *Journal of the American Psychoanalytic Association* 39 (1991): 45-70.

———. "Sadomasochism, Sexual Excitement, and Perversion." *Journal of the American Psychoanalytic Association* 39 (1991): 333-62.

Kessler, Suzanne. "The Medical Construction of Gender: Case Management of Intersexed Infants." *Signs* 16 (1990): 3-26.

Kikumura, Akemi. *Through Harsh Winters: The Life of a Japanese Immigrant Woman*. Novato, Calif.: Chandler & Sharpe, 1981.

Kincaid, Jamaica. *Annie John*. New York: Farrar, Straus & Giroux, 1983, 1984, 1985.

———. *Lucy*. New York: Farrar, Straus & Giroux, 1990.

Klein, Melanie. "Early Stages of the Oedipus Conflict" (1928). In *Love, Guilt and Reparation and Other Works*, pp. 186-98. New York: Delta, 1975.

———. "A Contribution to the Psychogenesis of Manic-Depressive States" (1935). In *Love, Guilt and Reparation*, pp. 262-89. *See* Klein, "Early Stages."

———. "Mourning and Its Relation to Manic-Depressive States" (1940). In *Love, Guilt and Reparation*, pp. 344-69. *See* Klein, "Early Stages."

———. "The Oedipus Conflict in the Light of Early Anxieties" (1945). In *Love, Guilt and Reparation*, pp. 370-419. *See* Klein, "Early Stages."

———. "Envy and Gratitude" (1957). In *Envy and Gratitude and Other Works*, pp. 176-235. New York: Delta, 1975.

Krieger, Susan. *The Mirror Dance*. Philadelphia: Temple Univ. Press, 1983.

Kris, Ernst. "The Personal Myth." *Journal of the American Psychoanalytic Association* 4 (1956): 653-81.

Lacan, Jacques. *Feminine Sexuality* (1966, 1968, 1975). Ed. Juliet Mitchell and Jacqueline Rose. New York: Norton, 1982.

Lakoff, Robin, and Raquel Scherr. *Face Value*. Boston: Routledge, 1984.

Lampl-de Groot, Jeanne. "The Evolution of the Oedipus Complex in Women" (1927). In *The Development of the Mind: Psychoanalytic Papers on Clinical and Theoretical Problems*, pp. 3-18. New York: International Universities Press, 1965.

Leonard, Marjorie R. "Fathers and Daughters: The Significance of 'Fathering' in the Psychosexual Development of the Girl." *International Journal of Psycho-Analysis* 47 (1966): 325-34.

Levy, Robert I. *Tahitians: Mind and Experience in the Society Islands*. Chicago: Univ. of Chicago Press, 1973.

Lewes, Kenneth. *The Psychoanalytic Theory of Male Homosexuality*. New York: Simon & Schuster, 1988.

Lindenbaum, Joyce P. "The Shattering of an Illusion: The Problem of Competition in Lesbian Relationships." *Feminist Studies* 11 (1985): 85-103.

Maccoby, Eleanor, and Carol Jacklin. *The Psychology of Sex Differences*. Stanford, Calif.: Stanford Univ. Press, 1974.

McDougall, Joyce. "Homosexuality in Women." In *Female Sexuality: New Psychoanalytic Views*, ed. Janine Chasseguet-Smirgel, pp. 171-212. Ann Arbor: Univ. of Michigan Press, 1970.

———. *Theatres of the Mind: Illusion and Truth on the Psychoanalytic Stage*. London: Free Association Books, 1986.

Mahler, Margaret S., Fred Pine, and Anni Bergmann. *The Psychological Birth of the Human Infant*. New York: Basic Books, 1975.

Martin, Karin. "Feminism, Sexual Subjectivity, and a History of Women's Orgasm in the West." Tutorial paper prepared for Sociology Preliminary Examinations, Univ. of California, Berkeley, 1991.

———. "Gender and Sexuality: Medical Opinion on Homosexuality, 1900-1950." *Gender and Society* 7 (1993): 246-60.

———. "Puberty, Sexuality, and the Self: Gender Differences in Adolescence." Ph.D. diss. Univ. of California, Berkeley, 1994.

Mernissi, Fatima. *Beyond the Veil: Male-Female Dynamics in a Modern Muslim Society*. Cambridge: Schenkman, 1975.

Michel, Frann. "After the World Broke: Cross-Gender Representation in Works by Willa Cather, William Faulkner, and Djuna Barnes." Ph.D. diss. University of California, Berkeley, 1990.

Mitchell, Juliet. "Eternal Divide." *The Times Higher Education Supplement* (London), 17 Nov. 1989, p. 20.

Money, John, and Anke Ehrhardt. *Man and Woman, Boy and Girl*. Baltimore, Md.: Johns Hopkins Univ. Press, 1972.

Moraga, Cherríe. "From a Long Line of Vendidas: Chicanas and Feminism." In *Feminist Studies/Critical Studies*, ed. Teresa de Lauretis, pp. 173-90. Madison: Univ. of Wisconsin Press, 1986.

Morgenthaler, Fritz. *Homosexuality, Heterosexuality, Perversion*. New York: Analytic Press, 1988.

Neumann, Erich. *The Great Mother*. 2d ed. Princeton, N.J.: Princeton Univ. Press, 1963.

Parsons, Anne. *Belief, Magic and Anomie*. New York: Free Press, 1969.

Person, Ethel S. "The Omni-Available Woman and Lesbian Sex: Two Fantasy Themes and Their Relationship to the Male Developmental Experience." In *The Psychology of Men*, ed. Gerald I. Fogel, Frederick M. Lane, and Robert S. Liebert, pp. 71-94. New York: Basic Books, 1986.

———. *Dreams of Love and Fateful Encounters: The Power of Romantic Passion*. New York: Norton, 1988.

Plaskow, Judith. *Standing Again at Sinai*. New York: Harper-Collins, 1990.

Quinn, Susan. *A Mind of Her Own: A Life of Karen Horney*. New York: Summit Books, 1987.

Reich, Annie. "Narcissistic Object Choice in Women." *Journal of the American Psychoanalytic Association* 1 (1953): 22-44.

Rich, Adrienne. *Of Woman Born: Motherhood as Experience and Institution*. New York: Norton, 1976.

———. "Compulsory Heterosexuality and Lesbian Existence." *Signs* 5 (1980): 631-60.

Roazen, Paul. *Helene Deutsch*. New York: Anchor, 1985.

Roiphe, Herman, and Eleanor Galenson. *Infantile Origins of Sexual Identity*. New York: International Universities Press, 1981.

Roth, Philip. *Portnoy's Complaint*. New York: Random House, 1983.

Rubin, Gayle. "The Traffic in Women: Notes on a 'Political Economy' of Sex." In *Toward an Anthropology of Women*, ed. Rayna Reiter, pp. 157-210. New York: Monthly Review Press, 1975.

Schafer, Roy. "Problems in Freud's Psychology of Women." *Journal of the American Psychoanalytic Association* 22 (1974): 459-85.

Slater, Philip. *The Glory of Hera: Greek Mythology and the Greek Family*. Boston: Beacon Press, 1968.

Smith-Rosenberg, Carroll. *Disorderly Conduct: Visions of Gender in Victorian America*. Oxford: Oxford University Press, 1985.

Socarides, Charles. *Homosexuality*. New York: Jason Aronson, 1978.

———. "A Unitary Theory of Sexual Perversions." In *On Sexuality*, ed. Thomas Karasu and Charles Socarides, pp. 161-88. New York: International Universities Press, 1979.

———. *The Preoedipal Origin and Psychoanalytic Therapy of Sexual Perversions*. New York: International Universities Press, 1988.

Stein, Arlene. "Three Models of Sexuality: Drives, Identities and Practices." *Sociological Theory* 7 (1989): 1-13.

———. "Sexuality, Generation and the Self: Constructions of Lesbian Identity in the 'Decisive' Generation." Ph.D. diss., Univ. of California, Berkeley, 1992.

———. "Sisters and Queers: The Decentering of Lesbian Feminism." *Socialist Review* 22 (1992): 33-55.

Stern, Daniel N. *The Interpersonal World of the Infant*. New York: Basic Books, 1985.

Stoller, Robert. *Perversion: The Erotic Form of Hatred*. New York: Pantheon, 1975.

———. *Sexual Excitement*. New York: Pantheon, 1979.

———. *Observing the Erotic Imagination*. New Haven: Yale Univ. Press, 1985.

Stolorow, Robert D., and Frank M. Lachman. *Psychoanalysis of Developmental Arrests*. New York: International Universities Press, 1980.

Strouse, Jean. *Alice James: A Biography*. New York: Bantam, 1989.

Tan, Amy. *The Joy Luck Club*. New York: G.P Putnam's Sons, 1989.

Thompson, Nellie. "Helene Deutsch: A Life in Theory." *Psychoanalytic Quarterly* 56 (1987): 317-53.

Thorne, Barrie. *Gender Play: Girls and Boys in School*. New Brunswick, N.J.: Rutgers Univ. Press, 1993.

"Toward the Further Understanding of Homosexual Women." Panel discussion; Abby Wolfson, reporter. *Journal of the American Psychoanalytic Association* 35 (1987): 165-73.

Walker, Alice. "In Search of Our Mothers' Gardens." In *Working It Out*, ed. Sara Ruddick and Pamela Daniels, pp. 93-102. New York: Pantheon, 1977.

Weeks, Jeffrey. *Sexuality*. London: Tavistock, 1986.

Young-Bruehl, Elizabeth. *Anna Freud*. New York: Summit, 1988.

Index